Rise and 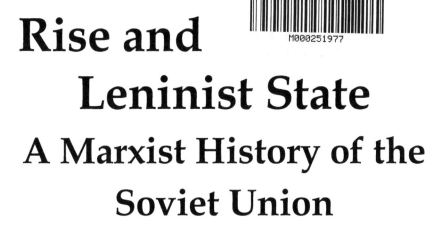 Leninist State
A Marxist History of the Soviet Union

Lenny Flank

Red and Black Publishers, St Petersburg, Florida

Library of Congress Cataloging-in-Publication Data

Flank, Lenny.
  Rise and fall of the Leninist state : a Marxist history of the Soviet Union / Lenny
Flank.
      p. cm.
  ISBN 978-1-934941-34-8
  1. Soviet Union--History. 2. Communism--Soviet Union--History. 3. Communism.
I. Title.
  DK266.F52 2008
  320.53'22--dc22

                                                                    2008021857

Red and Black Publishers, St Petersburg, Florida
Contact us at: redandblackpublishers@yahoo.com
Printed and manufactured in the United States of America

Contents

Preface

When Mikhail Gorbachev took office in 1985, it seemed incredible to assert that the Soviet Union was about to collapse from its own internal contradictions. The reactionary Chernenko government held the reins of power, the Polish Solidarity movement had been crushed, a new Cold War with the United States was brewing. The Russian bear seemed nearly invincible. Yet, by 1990, the Soviet Union was dead.

These events took the United States, and particularly the Left, by surprise. They shouldn't have. The roots of the Soviet collapse can be clearly seen in the economic experiments of the 1960's. In fact, the economic crises to which the "Gorbachev revolution" was a response can be traced back to the very structure of pre-Revolutionary Russia.

As a revolutionary Marxist, I think it is imperative that we examine the development of the Soviet Union, both in theory and in actual practice, and that we understand the historical and material circumstances which prompted that development. By doing so, we can in the future, I hope, avoid the mistakes and horrors inflicted upon revolutionary socialism by the Marxist-Leninists. I hope that we can transform socialism from a regimented work camp into a humanistic social whole.

Lenny Flank
June 2008

Introduction

In March 1985, Soviet Communist Party General Secretary Konstantin Chernenko, a staunch Old Guard conservative and Brezhnev protege, died and was replaced by Mikhail Gorbachev. Immediately after assuming power, Gorbachev announced plans to carry out sweeping reforms within the massive Soviet economic bureaucracy, and introduced free-market methods of monetary incentives and decentralized economic decision-making as methods of rejuvenating the stagnating Soviet economy. Gorbachev referred to this process as *perestroika*, or "restructuring".

In 1989, within the space of a few months, the Communist nations of Eastern Europe underwent a series of profound convulsions. Enthusiastically embracing *perestroika* and *glasnost*, the East Europeans rose en masse and drove the old Stalinist bureaucrats from power. Within months, the Leninist empire was dead.

The Western powers hailed these actions as a "new revolution", and happily declared that "communism is dead". Many leftists and radical theorists were thrown into a panic by the Gorbachev revolution and the collapse of the Soviet Union, declaring it to be a "crisis of Marxism".

In these discussions and disputes, the Western press and most leftist commentators on *perestroika* have accepted the Soviet Union's assertion that the Revolution of October 1917 that brought the Bolsheviks to power resulted in the overthrow of the capitalist order and its substitution by socialism, and that the Soviet Union was a communist country that operated according to the principles described by Karl Marx and Frederick Engels. Even those leftist critics who attacked the policies of the USSR have, for the most part, accepted the proposition that the Soviet Union started its development as a socialist country — they simply assert that this development has proceeded "abnormally".

This book seeks to examine the political and economic history of the Soviet Union from its birth in 1917 to its recent demise. This study will focus largely on the economic factors affecting the development of the Soviet Union, which both Marx and Lenin considered crucial to understanding the development of any human society. This is done not only in order to examine the Leninist state in its own terms, but also because Marx's emphasis on the economic factors provides the clearest picture of the development of the Leninist state. It is in the economy of the Communist state, not in its politics or ideology, that we find the seeds of its destruction.

Therefore, by examining the economic development of the USSR, we will see, not only why the Russian Revolution progressed as it did, but why it could not have progressed in any other way. We will see clearly the factors which demanded the establishment of the Leninist state, as well as the equally compelling reasons for its downfall.

This work, then, will present historical and economic examples which illustrate the following thesis: The most basic cause of the Russian Revolution was the urgent need to industrialize the economy and to throw off the restrictions of a largely feudalist agrarian economy. In the history of Western Europe, the transition from an agrarian feudal economy to an industrial capitalist one had been carried out by the rising bourgeoisie, acting in alliance with the peasantry and the working class.

The Western path of development had, however, been rendered impossible in Russia by the near-total domination of the Russian economy by foreign financial interests. This foreign domination both hindered the development of a native bourgeois class and limited the economic and political power this class was able to gather.

As a result of the bourgeoisie's weakness, the task of industrializing the Russian economy fell to the professional middle class, or petty bourgeoisie, which gathered Russia's meager economic resources and, using a rigid system of planned economic expansion, succeeded in producing the rudiments of an industrialized economy. This process necessitated a program of nationalization and confiscation, placing all economic resources in the hands of the state.

By the 1960's, however, the rigid central hierarchy which had enabled the economy to expand so rapidly through the 1930's had begun instead to restrict and limit its future growth. In an attempt to alleviate these problems, Kruschev began a program of relaxing central control over the planning process and of placing economic power in the hands of the individual enterprise managers. *Perestroika* was an expansion of this process.

This, however, demanded the delegation of more and more autonomy to the lower levels of the economic system, eventually giving the factory managers de facto control over the economy. At this point, decentralized production came to be in conflict with the central planning apparatus. The result was the overthrow of the Leninist centralized economy and the introduction of a capitalist economy based on the free market and private ownership over resources. The Communist state fell, and was replaced by a Western-style democratic republic.

To see where the Leninist state is heading, we must understand from where it has come. We therefore begin our study with an examination of the economic circumstances which produced the Soviet Union.

ONE: The Economics of Revolution (1800 to 1905)

The Bolshevik coup of October 1917 resulted in the birth of the revolutionary strategy known as Leninism. While the physical overthrow of the Tsarist government took place in 1917, the economic preconditions for the revolt had been steadily growing throughout the 1800's. To fully understand the success of the Leninist revolution, we must understand the preconditions which made it possible.

When Tsar Alexander II took the throne in 1855, Russia was in the midst of drastic changes. The old autocratic feudal system was rapidly disintegrating. The agriculturally-based economy was simply no longer suited to the needs of the population, while the development of manufacturing and industry was hampered by economic and political conditions. The majority of the population was composed of serfs and peasants, who lived in poverty while a small portion of the population, the landowners and the aristocracy, controlled most of the nation's resources.

Clearly, this situation could not be changed without a radical upheaval that would completely destroy the old feudal network. An examination of the economic trends within Russia during the 19th century reveals that such a change had already begun.

Trotsky, in his study of the Russian Revolution, points out, "The basic criterion of the economic level of a nation is the productivity of labor, which in its turn depends upon the relative weight of the industries in the general economy of the country."

Measured by this yardstick, the economic level of Russia by 1820 was low, but advances were being made. Small industries were developing in the towns and villages, while light industry was taking root in the peasant *mir*, or communal peasant farms. Economically, Russia was at the level that had been reached by Western Europe in the late 1600's. Like its European predecessors, Russian society was poised on the edge of a leap that would industrialize and mechanize its economy and, at the same time, revolutionize its political and social order. Engels points out that, in Europe as well as in Russia, this leap towards industrialization was vital:

Before capitalist production, i.e., in the Middle Ages, the system of petty industry generally prevailed, based upon the private property of the laborers in their means of production; in the country, the agriculture of the small peasant, freemen or serf; in the town, the handicrafts organized in guilds. The instruments of labor — land, agricultural implements, the work-shop, the tool — were the instruments of labor of single individuals, adapted for the use of one worker, and, therefore, of necessity, small, dwarfish, circumscribed. But for this very reason they belonged, as a rule, to the producer himself. To concentrate these scattered, limited means of production, to enlarge them, to turn them into the powerful levers of production of the present day —

this was precisely the historic role of capitalist production and of its upholder, the bourgeoisie.

By the 19th century, Russia's economy, still based on the feudalist agrarian activity typical of the period before capitalism, was unable to meet the needs of the population. Through necessity, the Russians were forced to increase the productivity of their labor. This could be done only in one way – the same way in which the Europeans had solved the same dilemma – the organization of individual industries into the factory system typical of capitalism. Engels, noting that the growing Russian bourgeoisie "has been making frantic exertions to develop its own capitalist production", pointed out in 1820 that further industrialization had become an economic necessity.

Between 1825 and 1855, the number of Russians employed in industry and manufacturing more than doubled, from 210,000 to 183,000. Nevertheless, the level of industrialization was still inadequate. This was made apparent during the war with France in 1853. While Russia was able to raise an army of 1.25 million, the country's industry and transportation networks were so weak that only 350,000 men could be brought to the front. The Tsarist government formed a committee in 1855 to study the possibility of constructing a network of railroads throughout the country. After the war, a group of Russian representatives met with European officials in Paris to seek help for Russian industrialization. Three French, one British and one Dutch bank agreed to finance the construction of a railroad system in Russia. Work began in 1868 and continued until 1874.

As the economic power of the manufacturing sector increased, so too did the political and economic power of the bourgeoisie which controlled it. The growing influence of the Russian middle class led to increasingly expansionistic military moves. While Tsar Alexander favored a period of pacifism to allow Russia to rebuild after the Crimean War, he was forced to give in to the demands of the military, supported by the infant merchant class. The east shore of the Caspian Sea had attracted several oil, salt and sulphur companies, and was annexed between 1857 and 1873. In 1860, the Chinese provinces of Amur and Ussuri were seized and transformed into the Russian Maritime Provinces.

By 1875, the Russian bourgeoisie had formed the so-called "Pan-Slav" movement, calling for the unity of all Slavs and the liberation of the Balkans from Austria-Hungary. Alexander II opposed the Pan-Slavists, but was unable to stop their influence. When agrarian revolts broke out in Herzegovina, Serbia pledged support for the rebellion and asked for Russian aid. Alexander refused, but prominent Pan-Slavists among the Russian bourgeoisie declared support. Both Serbia and Montenegro declared war on Turkey in July 1876, supported by 5,000 Russian volunteers.

Alexander, in an attempt to get out of a bad situation, offered to withdraw the Russians if Turkey would grant concessions to the Balkan states. The concessions never came, and Russia entered the war in April 1877. Turkey was defeated, but not before Russia lost the Bosporus straits to the British fleet.

Meanwhile, the industrialization program begun in 1855 received new emphasis from Tsar Nicholas II. During the 1890's, Nicholas authorized Finance Minister von Witte to begin a program to expand Russian manufacturing capacity. The results were phenomenal. In ten years, Russian production of pig iron went up 108%, at a time when German production rose only 72% and American production rose 50%. Russian steel and iron output leaped 116%, compared to 73% for Germany and 63% for the United States. Between 1890 and 1899, German coal production rose 52% and American output jumped 61%. During this period, Russian coal production leaped 131%.

By 1900, 34% of Russia's factories employed 500 or more workers, compared to only 14% of German factories. Russian factories employing over 1,000 workers made up 24% of the total, while only 8% of German factories employed over 1,000. By 1914, only 17.8% of the Russian workforce was employed in factories of 100 or less employees. By contrast, 35% of the American work force labored in enterprises of 100 or less employees. Only 17.8%

of American workers were in factories with 1,000 or more employees, while 41.4% of Russian workers were so employed.

This surge in economic growth, notes economist Marshall Goldman, was remarkable:

According to both Russian and Western sources, Russian growth between the early 1880's and 1913 was very impressive. It was in this brief 23-year period that Russia emerged from the ranks of the economically impoverished. By 1913, steel production was five times larger than it was in 1890. There was almost a tenfold increase in the mining of coal. The railroad network almost tripled in size. Especially notable was the building of the Trans-Siberian Railroad, one of the most impressive engineering accomplishments of the time.

Thus, concludes Goldman, Russia by 1915 was no longer the hopelessly backward nation it had been in 1820:

It is true that Russia before World War I was economically inferior to England, Germany and France, not to mention the United States. Even France produced more than double what Russia manufactured in 1923, and the figures were considerably higher for comparisons with Germany and England. But it is too much to say that Russia's economy was as backward as those of most of the countries of Asia and Africa today. Because of the statistical uncertainties involved, it is impossible to make an unreserved statement, but Russia in 1913 may have been economically superior to Japan and perhaps Italy. All three countries were early examples of what is today called a dual economy. A very modern sector existed simultaneously with a very primitive sector in both industry and agriculture.

This contradiction between a modern, developing economic sector and a primitive, idle sector was, in fact, a growing contradiction between the old feudalist economy and the growing capitalist system that would replace it. This growing industrial bourgeoisie would eventually unite itself with the peasantry and the workers and overthrow the feudal aristocracy that was hampering its development, just as the European monarchies had been deposed by the newly-developed bourgeoisie.

Yet, in Russia as in every Leninist state since, this did not happen. In each case of Leninist revolution, the native bourgeoisie proved itself incapable of overthrowing feudalism and fulfilling the "historic role" assigned to it by Marx and Engels — namely, that of concentrating the scattered means of production formed by the feudal state into large-scale industry. The Russian merchants were able to begin the process of industrialization, but were unable to complete it, or, what amounts to the same thing, overthrow the feudalist system that inhibited the manufacturing sector. Why, we are forced to ask, was the Russian bourgeoisie unable to complete the task which the European bourgeoisie had fulfilled?

The answer to this apparent paradox lies in the fact that Russia did not develop in a vacuum. As Russia's economic development progressed, the more economically advanced nations of the West began to involve themselves more and more in Russian internal development. The advanced capitalist countries saw in Mother Russia a vast source of cheap labor, plentiful raw materials and expanded markets, and fell upon her like wolves. The Western capitalists rolled over the infant Russian bourgeoisie, in an economic invasion that reduced the native merchant class to pawns and tools of the foreign financial interests. In the end, it was the West, not the Russian bourgeoisie, that began the industrialization process and slowly gathered real economic power.

Lenin was not blind to this process, and in fact described it in some detail, declaring this "economic imperialism" to be "the highest stage of capitalism". This economic onslaught, Lenin reasoned, would produce such a state of oppression in the "colonies" that they would, in desperation, be driven to revolt against the imperialist powers. This, Lenin concluded, would in turn provoke the proletariat of the imperialist countries to revolt in support of the colonies, leading to world-wide Communist revolution.

Lenin's theory of imperialism seemed to be coming to life in 19th century Russia. Economic domination by the West had produced the complete impotence of the Russian bourgeoisie and the domination of the Tsarist economy by the European powers. Trotsky pointed out that this domination was so compete that "Foreigners owned in general about 40% of all the stock capital in Russia, but in the leading branches of industry that percentage was still higher." Economist Maurice Dobbs adds, "The factories that existed were frequently foreign importations; foreign-owned, foreign-financed and staffed by foreign managerial and technical personnel."

This foreign investment had begun in earnest during the 1840's railroad boom. In fact, Russia's first major railroad line, from Moscow to St. Petersburg, was built between 1842 and 1851 by American firms using American capital. By 1847, foreign domination was so great that, of the 13.4 million rubles exported by Russia, only 2% came from Russian-owned industries. By 1898, Russia was exporting over 17.4 million rubles while importing only 13.3 million.

Since Russia was largely an agrarian economy, the major portion of the country's exports was made up of agricultural products. Between 1861 and 1865, the average export of grain was 76 million poods per year (a pood equals thirty-six pounds). By 1876, this had jumped to 257 million per year. Between 1894 and 1914, the output of wheat (the major export crop) rose 75%, while the output of rye (the primary crop for home consumption) did not increase significantly.

By 1914, over half of Russia's exports were made up of wheat and other foodstuffs. Another 36% was composed of industrial raw materials and semi-manufactured goods. During this time, almost half of Russia's imports were made up of raw materials not found in Russia (cotton, silk, wool and non-ferrous metals), while some 33% of imports were various types of manufactured products.

These figures demonstrate clearly the process of economic imperialism. Foreign powers systematically drained Russia of foodstuffs and available raw materials, and used cheap Russian unskilled labor to produce sub-assemblies which were shipped back to the home country for assembly and finally sold back to the Russians.

Given such a lucrative opportunity, it is no wonder that foreign investment in Russia was heavy. In 1901, the entire German electric industry had a capital of 233 million marks. Of this amount, 62 million were invested in Russia. In 1907, Rumanian oil fields attracted 185 million francs of foreign capital, of which 71 million came from Germany. In addition, four major Russian banks were completely dominated by German capital.

If this seems considerable, it is worth noting that investment by England, France and Belgium was almost double that of Germany. Five major Russian banks were controlled by French capital, while British financiers controlled the Russo-British Bank and the Commercial And Industrial Bank. Of the principle banks in St Petersburg, 55% of the capital was French-owned, 35% German and 10% British. Of this, about 10% was invested in Russian oil, mineral and metallurgical syndicates. About 42% of all the capital of the 18 largest banks in Russia was owned by foreign financiers. In fact, only 8 major Russian banks were actually controlled by Russian capital. Of all the foreign capital invested in Russia in 1914, 32% was owned by French financiers and 22% by British. Foreign industrialists owned or controlled 80% of Russia's oil, coal and metallurgical industries, and the primary coal-producing region, the Donetz Basin, was 50% foreign-owned.

This foreign domination was compounded by the fact that production within the industries themselves was concentrated in a small number of foreign-owned firms. A total of nine iron and steel plants, for instance, produced over 50% of Russia's pig iron output in 1913. Seven firms produced nearly 90% of the 1913 output of railroad rails, while six companies accounted for 60% of the oil output at the Baku oilfields.

Looking at these figures, it is not hard to see the enormous influence the Western powers enjoyed over the Russian economy. The tentacles of foreign domination reached into nearly every facet of Russian economic, political and social life.

Inextricably tied up with the increase in industrialization was the growth of the Russian city. In Europe during the Middle Ages, the cities had grown gradually as the introduction of industry concentrated the means of production in the urban areas. With the rapid industrialization brought about by the foreign economic invasion, however, the growth of the Russian city was greatly accelerated.

In 1812, only 4.4% of Russia's population lived in the cities. By 1897, this had increased to 13%. From 1870 to 1905, the population of Moscow increased 123%, and the increase was even larger in Odessa, Baku and Rostov. In 1905, 57% of all Russian factories and 58% of its workers were in the urban areas.

Russia was still, however, largely an agrarian nation. In the period between 1900 and 1915, 80% of the population lived in the rural areas. Only 17% of the work force was employed in industry. As of 1910, 66% of the factory workers in St Petersburg also rented land in the country, and some 20% of these still went back to the village *mir* every summer to help in the harvest. This link between town and country would become crucial to the events of 1917. It directly linked the problem of industrialization to the most explosive situation facing Russia — the agrarian revolution.

By the middle of the 19th century, it was becoming increasingly clear that the feudalist agricultural system was on the verge of collapse. Serf and peasant rebellions followed one after another, fueled by poverty, hunger and the appalling conditions of serfdom. The landed aristocracy, dependent on the serfs for their position of privilege, vigorously opposed the endless revolts. Both Alexander I and Nicholas I had made plans to abolish serfdom and thus pacify the Russian countryside, but both gave in to the opposition of the landed gentry. As researcher W.E. Mosse notes, "Orlov, Panin and their supporters in governmental spheres knew that liberation would mean the end of the existing social order and were determined to fight it to the end."

It was not until the growing Russian merchant class entered the picture that serious attention was turned to abolishing the feudal relationships. The bourgeoisie needed laborers for its factories and surplus grain to trade with the West, and the antiquated conditions in the agricultural sphere were making this impossible. It is, therefore, not surprising that the Russian merchants, led by the millionaire Kokorev, worked to support the abolition of serfdom and to improve the conditions among the Russian muzhik peasant farmers.

By the 1850's, Alexander II realized that the institution of serfdom was holding back the economic development of Russia as well as creating a politically unstable situation in the countryside. Realizing that the end of the feudal aristocracy was unavoidable, Alexander told a group of Moscow gentry in 1856, "I do not at the present intend to abolish serfdom, but, certainly, as you well know yourselves, the existing manner of owning serfs cannot remain unchanged. It is better to abolish serfdom from above than to await the time when it will begin to abolish itself from below."

After years of delays and peasant revolts, Alexander II abolished serfdom on March 3, 1861. He was already too late. By 1860, the power of the Russian bourgeoisie was eclipsing that of the gentry. By 1861, the industrialization program was in full swing and the interests of the Russian merchant class had already begun to replace those of the feudal landlords. The landed aristocracy had to be disbanded, along with the system of land ownership that supported it.

With this economic background, it is obvious why the Tsar's liberation benefited neither the gentry nor the muzhik, but the bourgeois elements in the countryside. The Emancipation was presented in two forms. The first option freed the serf and gave him the land he worked on, allowing him 49 years to pay the landlord the value of the land. In the second option, the freed serf received only one-fourth of the land to which he was entitled, but did not have to pay anything for it.

Only about 6% of the serfs chose the second option, the so-called "poverty lots", but these were concentrated in strategic areas. In areas where the land was poor and relatively infertile, the landlord was happy to give the land to the muzhik and take his money. In areas where land was valuable, however, the gentry often coerced the freed serfs into taking the poverty lots. This enabled the landlords to retain large holdings of valuable land, which could be rented out or worked by cheap labor to reap huge profits. In most cases, the landlords obtained their laborers from the "liberated" serfs, who were unable to feed themselves with the yields from their poverty lots. In essence, the serfs found themselves working under the same masters for pitiful pay.

Muzhiks who received the full share of land often found themselves in no better condition. Unable to afford either hired labor or modern farming equipment, most struggled to simply pay off their land, pay their taxes and make a living. The lot of the peasant in 1862 was, therefore, not much better than it had been in 1860.

Only one sector of the rural population benefittd from the terms of the Emancipation—the wealthier muzhiks who could afford to buy land, hire labor and use machinery. These peasants, dubbed kulaks ("fists") made up a small minority of Russian farms, but their economic power was considerable. In 1878, the kulaks, who composed only 13% of the peasantry, were considered by Tsarist government studies to be "well-provided" with land. Another 40% of the peasantry was "adequately provided", while a full 47% did not have enough land to sustain themselves. Consequently, by 1895, half of the peasantry had an "adequate supply" of bread, while a full 20% didn't have enough bread to feed themselves.

Conditions of poverty among the peasantry depressed the already stunted rural economy. By 1900, only about 25% of the arable land in Russia was under cultivation, compared to 40% of the available land in industrialized Germany. Russian yield per acre was only 25% that of the United Kingdom and 50% that of France. In Russia, one farmer cultivated an average of three acres, while one person in the United States was able to cultivate an average of thirteen acres.

By the beginning of the 20th century, the power of the kulak had grown considerably. After the establishment of the Peasant's Land Bank in 1883, the kulaks flocked to buy up the available land. Of all the purchases made through the Land Bank, 56% involved lots of 270 acres or more, and these purchases were made by less than 5% of the peasantry. By 1905, the top 10% of the peasantry owned 35% of all Russian farm area, each farm averaging 55 acres in size. The poorest 10% of muzhiks owned only 1% of total farm area, with each farm averaging just ten acres each.

In addition to controlling most of the land, the kulaks also controlled most of the farm machinery. In pre-revolutionary Russia, only 4% of farms had a reaper for use. Only 3% had a threshing machine and only 1% had a mower. While the average muzhik could produce only 9.7 bushels per acre of spring wheat, the kulak, with his superior equipment, was able to produce 11.5 bushels per acre. The average output of rye, the primary food crop, was 12.4 bushels per acre; the kulaks were able to produce 15.2 bushels per acre.

The inevitable result of this concentration was to produce wealth and prosperity for the kulaks and landowners, and increasing poverty and hunger among the muzhiks. The only solution, as the peasant saw it, was to own his own land. Since this was beyond the economic means of most of the peasantry, the only alternative was to revolt and seize the land forcibly. As Trotsky put it, "Choking in the narrowness of his land area, under the smarting whip of the treasury and the market, the muzhik was inexorably forced to attempt to get rid of the landlord once and for all." It was these feelings that ultimately produced the Revolutions of 1905 and 1917.

Shaken by the 1905 revolt, Stolypin began to push his land reform program in 1906. This was designed to allow the muzhik to drop out of the communal mir and buy his own farm, thus, the Tsarist government hoped, increasing productivity and stability in the rural areas. The solution, Stolypin thought, was to "wager not on the needy and the drunken, but on the strong—the sturdy individual proprietor."

However, like the Tsar's Emancipation, Stolypin's land reform was a case of too little, too late. It did nothing to decrease the power of the kulaks, who continued to exercise economic power. It also did little to placate the peasantry, which had long since tired of waiting for government reforms to give them land. Instead of promoting peace in the countryside, Stolypin's reforms only pointed out more clearly the crushing circumstances surrounding the muzhik.

By 1917, the contradictions between the rising industrial bourgeoisie and the old landed feudal aristocracy had reached the breaking point. The cities were already undergoing the industrialization necessary for capitalist production, and the kulaks had introduced capitalist methods into the agrarian sector. The Russian merchant class had already become powerful enough to influence foreign policy and propose internal economic programs. In every sphere, it appeared that Russia was about to make the change from a feudalist society to a capitalist one.

In August 1871, Marx examined conditions in Russia and foresaw the coming attempt by the Russian bourgeoisie to seize power:

> There is a revolution coming in Russia, however, slowly but surely. There are two classes that are greatly discontented with the recent abolition of serfdom—the laborer, whose position has not been in the least improved by it, and the smaller nobility, who have been ruined by it—and these two elements, once they can be induced to work together, will overthrow that tyrannical form of government easily when the first weak Tsar succeeds to the throne.

In 1877, Marx added, in a letter to a friend in America, "Russia . . . has long been on the threshold of an upheaval. . . . The upheaval will begin . . . with some playing at constitutionalism. . . . If Mother Nature is not particularly unfavorable to us, we shall yet live to see the fun."

Unfortunately for Marx, Mother Nature was indeed unkind. Marx died in 1883, some 34 years before the success of the Russian bourgeois revolution which he described.

TWO: Revolution
(1825 to 1917)

Throughout the 1800's, the social and economic development of Russia closely paralleled that of Europe prior to the Industrial Revolution. Russia, like France and Britain before it, seemed to be moving from a feudalist economy to capitalism. Industry had been increasing for years, capitalist types of agriculture had been established and were growing, and the political power of the Russian merchant class, while not total, was increasing. All that remained was for the Russian merchant class to sweep the outdated Tsarist hierarchy out of the way and build a framework under which capitalism could flourish in Russia. This transition, writes Engels, was necessary:

> The mode of production peculiar to the bourgeoisie, known, since Marx, as the capitalist mode of production, was incompatible with the feudal system, with the privileges it

conferred upon individuals, entire social ranks and local corporations, as well as with the hereditary ties of subordination which constituted the framework of its social organization. The bourgeoisie broke up the feudal system and built upon its ruins the capitalist order of society, the kingdom of free competition, personal liberty, the equality, before the law, of all commodity owners, and all the rest of the capitalist blessings. Thenceforth the capitalist mode of production could develop in freedom.

Pre-revolutionary Russia seemed to be treading the same path. In fact, pointed out the Russian Marxist Sergei Bulgakov:

Russia rapidly approximates West European culture and loses its former characteristics of an exclusively peasant and crude country. . . . Every new factory, every new industrial enterprise, carries us forward, increasing the numbers of people capable of intellectual Europeanization.

Yet, in 1917, after a year of revolution. Russia was controlled, not by the bourgeoisie, but by the "proletarian party" of Lenin. What had happened to transform the expected bourgeois revolution into Lenin's "socialist" one?

Marx himself provides the starting point in solving this question. Marx writes:

The feudal aristocracy was not the only class whose conditions of existence pined and perished in the atmosphere of modern bourgeois society. The medieval burghers and the small farmer proprietors were the precursors of the modern bourgeoisie. In those countries that are but little developed, these two classes still vegetate side by side with the rising bourgeoisie.

In the social development of Europe, these two classes, the rural peasants and the urban artisans, had joined ranks with the rising bourgeoisie to help overthrow the feudal monarchies. In doing so, however, these petty bourgeois classes brought about their own destruction, since the bourgeoisie's methods of manufacture quickly overtook and crushed them; the petty bourgeoisie and, especially, the peasantry, after serving the interests of the bourgeoisie by ridding it of the feudal system, were themselves destroyed as classes and were placed under the domination of the merchant class.

In 1917, Russia, too, contained these petty bourgeois elements, in the form of the intellectual professionals and the small urban enterprises. Like their European counterparts, the Russian petty bourgeoisie opposed the Tsarist monarchy, and stood ready to aid the merchant class in destroying the feudal system. But, in the case of Russia, the bourgeoisie failed in its bid to replace the old feudal apparatus with the capitalist mode of production. The reasons for this failure are crucial to an understanding of Leninist revolutions. In order to understand how the Leninist party was able to make the revolution, it is necessary to understand why the native merchant class was unable to make one.

In Russia, by 1917, Marxist and socialist thought had been circulating for over half a century. Among the intelligentsia, capitalism and all of its evils had been subjected to harsh criticism, and ideas were being tossed about to consider how Russia could skip the capitalist "stage" and perhaps jump directly to socialism. In their rhetoric and agitation, then, most of Russia's revolutionaries fought against, not only the decaying Tsarist state, but also the rising bourgeoisie that would, according to Marx, replace it.

In addition, both the peasantry and the proletariat saw daily signs of capitalist oppression, in the form of low wages, high rents and horrible working conditions. This, Trotsky points out, tended to alienate both the workers and the peasantry from the Russian merchant class:

> The incapacity of the bourgeoisie for political action was immediately caused by its relation to the proletariat and the peasantry. It could not lead after it workers who stood hostile in their everyday life, and had

early learned to generalize their problems. But it was likewise incapable of leading after it the peasantry, because it was entangled in a web of interest with the landlords, and dreaded a shake-up of property relations in any form.

The long years of domination by foreign capital had also stunted the growth of indigenous industry and robbed it of all its political and economic influence. While it was in the interests of the Russian merchant class to overthrow the Tsar and assert its own class interests, it was in the interests of the foreign dominators to prevent this, and to control and stunt the Russian bourgeoisie.

Trotsky tries to explain the economic isolation and political impotence of the Russian bourgeoisie in this way:

The social character of the Russian bourgeoisie and its political physiognomy were determined by the condition of origin and the structure of Russian industry. The extreme concentration of this industry alone meant that between the capitalist leaders and the masses there was no hierarchy of transitional layers. To this we must add that the proprietors of the principle industries, banking and transport enterprises, were foreigners, who realized on their investment not only the profits drawn from Russia, but also a political influence in foreign parliaments and so not only did not forward the struggle for Russian parliamentarism, but often opposed it. . . . Such are the elementary and irremovable causes of the anti-popular character of the Russian bourgeoisie. Whereas in the dawn of its history it was too unripe to accomplish a Reformation, when the time came for leading revolution, it was overripe.

In reality, when the time came for the Russian bourgeoisie to make its revolution, it was not, as Trotsky writes, "overripe"; rather, it had been so weakened by internal opposition and foreign domination that it was simply not strong enough to make its own revolution, and could not begin the process of economic development which had been carried out in Western Europe. This weakness on the part of the indigenous bourgeoisie raises a question that every Leninist revolution has attempted to answer; in the absence of a well-defined merchant class, what social class is able to overthrow feudalism?

In Europe, the bourgeoisie had triumphed over the monarchies and, in the Industrial Revolution, had expanded its economic powers to global proportions. By 1917, the strength of any nation could clearly be seen to lie in the strength of its industrial sector. But Russia in 1917, like every other Leninist nation, found itself in the awkward position of requiring revolution to bring about this industrialization, but lacking a merchant class of sufficient strength to brink about this revolution. As Yugoslavian Communist Milovan Djilas writes:

> The countries which were not yet industrialized ... found themselves in a dilemma. They had either to become industrialized, or to discontinue active participation on the stage of history, turning into captives of the developed countries and their monopolies, thus doomed to degeneracy. Local capital and the class and parties representing it were too weak to solve the problems of rapid industrialization. In these countries, revolution became an inescapable necessity, a vital need for the nation, and only one class could bring it about — the proletariat, or the revolutionary party representing it.

Yet if, as Djilas asserts, the proletariat is the only other class capable of bringing about the required revolution, how are nations in which the working class is nonexistent or at best embryonic able to accomplish that revolution? The proletariat in Russia in 1917 composed only a small minority of the population, and the percentage is even smaller in China, Southeast Asia and other Leninist nations. In such nations, one may ask, what class brought about the revolution, and how?

In Russia in 1917, there was only one other class that could benefit from the overthrow of feudalism and imperialism — the petty bourgeoisie, represented by the professional intelligentsia and the small businesses in the cities. In addition, the peasantry was politically active. In every Leninist revolt, the primary force behind the revolution is the countryside, not the city, and the peasantry, not the proletariat. Standing ready to fight by the side of the bourgeoisie in the struggle against feudalism, only the petty bourgeoisie is capable of continuing the struggle in the absence of a well-developed industrial class. And only the peasantry is able to stand with the petty bourgeoisie in opposing the weak and impotent bourgeoisie. Marx writes:

> In countries . . . where the farmers constitute far more than half of the population, it was natural that writers who sided with the proletariat against the bourgeoisie should use, in their criticism of the bourgeois regime, the standard of the farmer and petty bourgeoisie, and from the standpoint of these intermediate classes should take up the cudgels for the working class. Thus arose petty-bourgeois socialism.

In this passage, Marx foresees perfectly the revolutionary strategy of every Leninist party. While the bourgeoisie of Europe adopted the standpoint of the peasantry to win it as an ally in the struggle against the monarchy, the Russian petty bourgeoisie adopted the standpoint of the proletariat and the peasantry in order to win them over to the struggle against Tsarism.

Thus, Trotsky is not completely correct when he writes:

> The peasantry . . . could never of its own force have achieved the agrarian democratic revolution — that is, its own revolution. It had to have leadership. For the first time in world history the peasant was destined to find a leader in the person of the worker. In that lies the fundamental, and you may say the whole, difference between the Russian Revolution and all those preceding it.

In fact, the proletariat did not, as Trotsky supposes, lead the revolution. The Russian Revolution was led by the petty bourgeoisie, the intellectual "professional revolutionaries", who co-opted the interests of both the workers and the peasantry. It is this alliance between the petty bourgeoisie, the workers and the muzhiks that make Leninist revolution unique. Since the peasantry provided most of the physical power behind the revolutionary forces, Trotsky is correct when he notes;

> If the agrarian problem, as a heritage from the barbarianism of the old Russian history, had been solved by the bourgeoisie, if it could have been solved by them, the Russian proletariat could not possibly have come to power in 1917. . . . That is the essence of 1917.

The petty bourgeoisie was not, however, the only revolutionary class in Russia, and the October Revolution was not the only revolutionary movement. Before the Bolshevik victory, other revolutionary groups had tried and failed to topple Tsarist feudalism.

The first serious challenge to the autocracy came in December 1825, when a group of Army officers failed in an attempted coup. The Decembrists, as they were called, wanted to push Russia further along the path of modernization and to limit the power of the Tsar, but they also wanted to maintain the domination of the landed aristocracy. Without any mass support, the Decembrists had no chance of instituting any real social changes.

In 1830, revolts in Poland against Russian rule were put down by Tsarist troops, and Russian bullets quelled rebellions in Hungary in 1848 and Poland again in 1863. Between 1857 and 1861, waves of student protests in Russian universities supported the Polish and Hungarian rebellions. Several underground newspapers appeared calling for a constituent assembly to seize power from the Tsar and move Russia towards socialism. These insurrections soon spread into the Tsarist Army, where, a foreign observer noted in 1861, "From General to Major, all are reliable but of limited intelligence; from Major to Sergeant-Major, all are unreliable. The common soldier is unpredictable, and will follow whoever influences him."

In May 1862, four Army officers and two non-commissioned officers were arrested for passing out "subversive literature" and for "lying" about the Tsar. Three of them were condemned to death. At the same time, to halt the flow of critical literature, Alexander II imposed a heavy censorship and exiled radical leaders.

Just three years after liberating the serfs, Alexander, in an attempt to appease the masses calling for a constituent assembly, signed laws establishing the zemstvo, an elected local self-government. In reality, the zemstvo were dominated by the nobility and overseen by the Tsarist bureaucracy. The zemstvo were free only to handle local education, and managed to make large gains in this area between 1871 and 1887, but by 1897 only 21% of Russia's population was literate. It wasn't until 1908 that education became free and compulsory.

In December 1865, the St Petersburg zemstvo demanded the creation of a central zemstvo to act as a Constituent Assembly. In response, Alexander had the zemstvo disbanded and its leaders exiled.

The first assassination attempt came on April 16, 1866, when a minor nobleman named Karakozov fired a gun at the Tsar. Karakozov was hanged, but not before he declared that many government officials wished to overthrow Alexander.

Shaken by the attempt, Alexander nevertheless told an audience, "I suppose that you consider that I refuse to give up any of my powers from motives of petty ambition. I give you my imperial word that, this very minute, at this very table, I would sign any constitution you like, if I felt that this would be for the good of Russia. But I know that, if I were to do so today, tomorrow Russia would fall to pieces."

A young Pole named Berezowski apparently disagreed, and tried to shoot Alexander during a state visit to Paris in 1867.

At about this time the first underground revolutionary group was formed. Calling itself V Narod ("to the people"), it was largely composed of students who had been expelled from the universities during the rebellions of 1869-1873. The movement was temporarily broken up in 1874, when two groups of 193 and 50 were arrested, but had already re-formed by the time the first group went on trial in February 1877. Of the 193 arrested, 153 were acquitted, and the rest received light sentences. Alexander himself increased most of the sentences, and placed many of those acquitted in "administrative exile".

Another trial in 1878 gave the Tsar cause for greater alarm. After a veteran V Narod member, Bogoliubov, was arrested in a St Petersburg demonstration in December 1876, he refused to salute Trepov, the Police Chief, and was ordered flogged. Several revolutionary groups called for vengeance on Trepov, and, in January, Vera Zasulich succeeded in wounding him. At her trial, Zasulich was acquitted, with even the government officials at the trial applauding the verdict. In desperation, the Tsar declared that any further revolutionary attacks would be tried by military tribunals rather than civilian courts.

The threat had little effect. In 1878, Mezentsev, the head of the Third Division security police, was shot. In 1879, Prince Kropotkin was killed, and an attempt was made on Drentela, who had replaced Trepov. In April 1879, a member of the group Zemya I Volya ("Land and Liberty"), acting without the organization's knowledge, fired five shots at the Tsar.

Soloviev's attempt aggravated the dissension already raging within Zemya I Volya, eventually leading to a split within the group. The more pacifists members of Zemya I Volya formed a group known as Chornoi Peredel ("Black Partition"), a peaceful propaganda group, while the militants formed the Narodnaya Volya ("People's Will"), a terrorist group that sought to overthrow the Tsar and construct a socialist state around the peasant *mir*. In response to the wave of assassination attempts, Alexander ignored the advice of his cabinet, who favored giving publicly-elected officials a role in the government, and instead put all government functions under a Supreme Committee headed by General Loris. Loris, in an attempt to streamline the anti-terrorist police, ended the autonomy of the Third Division and formed a single political police unit, known as Okhrana. Later, thinking that the revolt had died out, Loris disbanded the Supreme Council and appointed himself Minister of the Interior.

But the revolt had not died out. On September 7, 1879, the Central Executive Committee of the Narodnaya Volya formally sentenced Alexander II to death. Weeks later, an attempt was made to blow up the railroad car carrying the Tsar from the Crimean Peninsula to St Petersburg. After several bungled tries, however, the group succeeded only in blowing apart an advance baggage car.

In January 1880, a Narodnaya Volya newspaper informed Alexander that his death sentence would be "pardoned" if he agreed to the formation of a Constituent Assembly. After that, the group managed to set off a cache of explosives in the Winter Palace, killing forty Cossack Guards.

On March 11, 1881, as the Narodnaya Volya was making plans to blow up the Tsar along with an entire St Petersburg street, the group's leader, Zhelinbov, was arrested. The arrest did not, however, end the group's plans. Two days later, Alexander II was killed by a bomb tossed at his feet by a Narodnaya Volya assassin. Hours before, Alexander had signed a decree establishing a provisional legislative body made up of zemstvo representatives and government officials.

Alexander II's succession by his son, Alexander III, did little to end the unrest. Conditions in the rural areas were worsened by the famines of 1891-1892, and strikes broke out in Petersburg in 1896. By 1901, a new revolutionary group had been formed among the peasantry. Calling itself the Social Revolutionary Party, the group carried on the program of the Narodnaya Volya, including the use of terror and assassination.

After Alexander III's death in 1894, Tsar Nicholas II assumed the throne, but was equally unable to contain the growing number of revolutionary groups. In the late 1890's, a former member of the Chornoi Peredel named Giorgi Plekhanov had formed a group called Emancipation of Labor, Russia's first avowedly Marxist revolutionary party. By 1903, the Emancipation of Labor group had spawned an offshoot called the Russian Social Democratic Party, and Vladimir Ilyich Lenin had established himself as head of the RSDP.

During this time, other revolutionary groups were making their appearance. The Constitutional Democrats, or Kadets, were formed in 1903. Headed by Miliukov, Vinaver and Shatsky, members of the Russian bourgeoisie, the Kadets advocated the overthrow of the Tsar and the establishment of a constitutional republic with a Western-style government and civil liberties.

In 1903, the Russian Social Democratic Party split into two factions; the Mensheviks ("minority"), who favored a period of bourgeois capitalism to pave the way for socialism, and the Bolsheviks ("majority"), who favored moving directly from feudalism to socialism. The United Social Democratic Internationalist Party, headed by the writer Maxim Gorki, was not connected to the RSDP, but favored the Menshevik view. The last of the major parties, the Populist Socialists, or Trudoviki, was a nationalist peasant party headed by Alexander Kerensky.

A myriad of minor parties had also arisen to demand an end to the Tsarist government. These included the Polish Socialist Party, the Social Democratic Party of Poland and Lithuania, the Jewish Socialist Bund, the Armenian Social Democracy, the Armenian Revolutionary Federalists, the Lettish Social Democratic League, the Lettish Social Democratic Labor Party, the Finnish Labor Party, the Finnish Party of Active Resistance, the Georgian Federation of Socialist Revolutionaries, the Ukrainian Revolutionary Party and the Lithuanian Social Democratic Party.

This increase in revolutionary groups was accompanied by an increase in revolutionary violence. Many of these acts were carried out by students who favored the revolutionary views of the muzhiks and the Social Revolutionaries. In 1901, Bogolepev, the Tsarist Minister of Education, was shot. Minister of the Interior

Sipyagin was shot in 1902, and his successor, Phleve, was killed by a bomb in 1901. The Tsar's uncle, Grand Duke Sergei, was shot and killed in 1905.

Increasingly, the Russian bourgeoisie was becoming the most influential of the revolutionary classes. When Count von Witte rose to the position of President of the Council of Ministers in 1905, he immediately began to push for a program of industrialization, government subsidies, tax reform and trade tariffs. Von Witte was enthusiastically supported by the Russian merchant class.

Meanwhile, the Tsarist Government was facing increasing opposition. A general strike in Odessa in 1903 quickly spread throughout southern Russia. Within a year, the zemstvo began to clamor for increased autonomy. By 1904, discontent within Russia had become nearly universal.

Clearly, by 1904, the battle lines had been drawn. On one side stood the Tsar and the entire feudal aristocracy. On the other stood the Russian bourgeoisie and its allies, the peasantry and the urban working class. The revolution that would sweep away the Tsar and place the merchant class in power was only a matter of time. Russia, it appeared, was about to undergo its "1789". The revolutionaries needed only the proper spark to set them off.

The catalyst came on February 8, 1904, when the Japanese attacked the Russian fleet at Port Arthur, igniting the Russo-Japanese War. Nicholas II seized on the war as a method of rallying his volatile country into unity in a patriotic war. With a quick victory over Japan, he reasoned, the Russian people would once again rally around the Motherland and the Tsar.

Nicholas' hopes were quickly dashed. Instead of winning a quick victory, the Russian Army was routed and humiliated. The drain on the economy caused by the war produced shortage, poverty and famine that fueled the discontent in both the cities and the countryside.

As the situation dragged on, the Russian bourgeoisie openly broke with the Tsarist government. Between 1904 and 1905, the millionaire Morozov donated 2,000 rubles a month to both factions of Lenin's Social Democrats, while Prince Obolenski became a contributor to the RSDP newspaper Iskra ("The Spark") before joining the Kadets. At least four other princes openly embraced the bourgeoisie's program of liberalism.

The fire finally started on January 9, 1905, when Father George Gapon, who headed a police-sanctioned labor union (designed to deflect working class anger from the Tsar to the merchant class), led almost a quarter of a million of his followers on a march to the Winter Palace to ask for concessions from the Tsar. The procession was stopped by troops, who opened fire into the crowd, killing hundreds and wounding perhaps thousands more. With these shots, the Tsarist regime lost all of its popular support, and "Bloody Sunday" became the rallying cry of the revolution.

Within weeks, strikes had broken out all over Russia. The vanguard of the revolutionary movement was St Petersburg. Since trade unions were illegal, the striking workers needed a central body to plan and coordinate the strikes. The Menshevik faction of the RSDP, led by Trotsky, responded by forming a soviet ("council") of worker representatives to direct the Petersburg rebellion. The Soviet of Worker's Delegates, which had begun as a mere strike committee, soon grew in scope and in power. As other soviets were organized in other cities and among the peasantry, they became local governmental powers, setting policies and enforcing their own decrees. At the height of the revolution, delegates from the largest soviets were making plans to form a Central Soviet to serve as a provisional government.

As the de facto government, the St Petersburg soviet enjoyed considerable support, particularly among the Russian bourgeoisie. The General Strike called for by the Soviet was endorsed by the Kadets, who were dominated by the merchant class. In fact, many members of the bourgeoisie financed Social Democratic and Social Revolutionary newspapers, and striking workers were often given half or even full pay during the time they were on strike.

By the middle of October 1905, Russia was completely paralyzed. The General Strike had virtually ended industrial production, while the peasantry had taken to burning manor houses and seizing land.

In a letter, Nicholas II described the situation:

> There were only two ways open; to find an energetic soldier and crush the rebellion by sheer force. . . . That would mean rivers of blood, and in the end we should be where we had started. . . . The other way out would be to give the people their civil rights, freedom of speech and press, and also to have all laws confirmed by a state duma -- that would of course be a constitution. . . . We discussed it for two days and in the end, invoking God's help, I signed.

On October 17, Nicholas signed a reform measure known as the October Manifesto. The Manifesto established a representative legislature, known as the Duma, and guaranteed civil liberties and a constitution. The President of the Council of Ministers, von Witte, was placed at the head of the constitutional government.

Thus, it would appear, the Russian Revolution was over. The bourgeoisie, aided by the peasantry and the workers, had deposed the monarchy and now stood at the head of a republican government. As in the history of Europe, the institutions of feudalism had been replaced by the institutions of capitalism.

But this was not yet to be. The feudalist aristocracy had been staggered, but not felled. While von Witte worked to carry out the October Manifesto, Trepov, in charge of Russia's police forces, worked equally hard to crush the revolution. The result, as Lenin described it, was a deadlock: "Tsarism is no longer able to suppress the revolution, the revolution is still unable to destroy Tsarism."

Trotsky bitterly wrote:

> So a constitution is granted. Freedom of assembly is granted but the assemblies are surrounded by the military. Freedom of

speech is granted, but the censorship exists after as before. Freedom of knowledge is granted, but the universities are occupied by troops. Inviolability of the person is granted, but the prisons are overflowing with the incarcerated: Witte is given to us, but Trepov remains to us. A constitution is given, but the autocracy remains. Everything is given — and nothing is given.

It was this dissatisfaction with the October Manifesto that produced the first split between the Russian bourgeoisie and its proletarian and agrarian allies. After calling off the General Strike, the St Petersburg Soviet began to carry out its own governmental functions, including its own censorship apparatus. In its first purely proletarian action, the Soviet attempted to set and enforce its own eight-hour working day provisions. This instantly brought opposition from the merchants and the government of von Witte.

When revolts broke out in November at the Kronstadt fortress and in Poland, Witte responded by executing the Kronstadt leaders and by declaring a state of siege in Poland. The Petersburg Soviet retaliated by calling for another general strike. But the Russian working class, now lacking the support of the bourgeoisie, was not strong enough to take on the whole of society, and the strike died out in failure.

As the progressive movement ground to a halt, the forces of reaction went on the offensive. Pro-Tsarist groups formed terror and assassination squads to combat the revolutionary organizations. Strikers responded by arming themselves with pistols, daggers, clubs and brass knuckles.

By December 1905, the reaction was strong enough to attack the revolutionary Soviets directly. On December 9, the Chairman of the Petersburg Soviet, Khrustalev, was arrested. The Soviet responded by calling on workers to refuse all payments to the government and to withdraw all money from the banks. Faced with a potential financial catastrophe, the government arrested the entire Executive Committee a week later.

Before being disbanded, the Soviet called for another general strike. The St Petersburg workers, lacking effective weapons, held no hope of defeating the Tsarist troops, and called off the strike. The Moscow workers, however, threw up barricades and, armed only with primitive weapons, held out against the Army for a week. With this action, the Revolution of 1905 came to an end.

A study of the class interactions during the 1905 Revolution points out several trends that would become important in 1917. In many ways, the course of the 1905 revolt would be duplicated in the February Revolution.

The 1905 uprising, like the 1917 Revolution, proceeded in two phases. In the first phase, the Russian bourgeoisie, aided by the petty bourgeoisie, the peasantry and the workers, forced the Tsar to grant a Duma and a constitution and, in effect, transformed Russia from a feudal state to a capitalist one.

Once the bourgeoisie had apparently claimed victory, however, the revolution entered its second phase. The merchant class found itself to be too weak to hold on to the power it has just conquered for itself, and its allies then became its enemies. In 1905, the petty bourgeoisie, the peasantry and the working class stood ready to seize control of the Revolution, but lacked the support of the Army. Unable to defeat the forces of reaction at the barricades, the revolutionary masses fell and the Revolution was defeated.

To the Tsarist government, the most frightening threat had come, not from the urban workers, but from the rural peasantry. The peasants had demonstrated that they cared for neither industrialization nor foreign trade — they wanted only land. This was illustrated by a group of muzhiks who looted and destroyed a sugar factory in Tchernigov province, saying, "We don't need the factory. We need the land on which it stands."

To combat this growing restlessness in the countryside, Nicholas turned to Stolypin's land reform program. On November 9, 1906, a law was passed allowing the muzhik to borrow money from the state to buy pieces of the communal mir. Stolypin defended the program by arguing, "The natural counterweight to the communal principle is in individual ownership; the small owner is the nucleus on which rests all stable order in the state."

In fact, the program only strengthened the growing capitalist forces in Russia, by allowing the kulaks to buy up most of the land thus freed. To Lenin, who hoped to skip from feudalism directly to socialism, this was unacceptable:

> If Stolypin's policy is continued . . . then the agrarian structure of Russia will become completely bourgeois, the stronger peasants will acquire almost all the allotments of land, agriculture will become capitalist and any "solution" to the agrarian problem — radical or otherwise — will become impossible under capitalism.

Nevertheless, the land reform was carried out, even after Stolypin was shot by a student revolutionary in 1911. Between 1906 and 1916, about 6.2 million peasant families out of 16 million eligible applied for loans to buy their own land and drop out of the *mir*. As Lenin feared, this strengthened the capitalist elements among the peasantry. As Prince Troubetskoy noted, "In the country a very powerful petty bourgeoisie is arising, in its whole make and essence alien alike to the ideas of the united nobility and to the socialist dreams."

After the 1905 Revolution failed to provide the muzhiks with land, the peasantry took its demands to the Duma. The peasant delegate Petrichenko told the Duma, "No matter how long you debate, you won't create a new planet — that means you'll have to give us the land." Turning to the political representatives of the landed aristocracy, he thundered, "Gentlemen of the gentry, you have stolen our land. We have come here not to buy it, but to take it."

It was all, however, a hollow exercise. The Duma, in which the merchant class had placed its hopes, had only a paper existence.

Many of the revolutionary parties suspected that the newly-formed Duma would be nothing more than a figurehead. During the general strike, most of the socialist parties favored boycotting the Duma elections and continuing the insurrection. After the Revolution died out and the Duma was set up, these same parties objected to the unequal voting system, in which the delegates of the bourgeoisie and the aristocracy had more representative power than those of the peasantry and the working class. The Social Revolutionaries and the Bolshevik faction of the Social Democrats refused to take part in the elections. Only the Mensheviks, realizing that the hopes of the people centered around the Duma, refused to boycott and won several seats. As a result of the boycott, the First Duma was dominated by 190 Kadets and 94 Trudoviks.

The merchant class delegates of the Duma immediately attempted to transform its powers into those of a Western-style parliament, with full legislative powers. The Kadet delegation demanded full Duma control over the budget and state fiscal matters, while the Trudoviks pushed for a new land redistribution program.

Nicholas reacted by disbanding the Duma in July 1906. The delegates, after calling for a general strike, fled to Finland and issued a manifesto calling for resistance. While the urban proletariat, still licking its wounds after the 1905 strikes, ignored the Duma's call, the peasantry erupted with riots and violence. The rebellions were put down by Tsarist troops. In a move designed to placate the countryside and prevent further outbreaks, Nicholas ordered elections for a new Duma, after first barring the candidacy of those who had signed the Finland Manifesto. This time, the socialist parties, realizing that the Duma provided a legal forum for agitation and propaganda, participated in the elections and won a bloc of seats.

It was an empty victory. The Tsarist government demanded the expulsion of the more "radical" of the delegates, including the Bolsheviks and Social Revolutionaries. When the Second Duma refused to expel the delegates, Stolypin ordered it dissolved on

June 16, 1907. To prevent the election of more "radicals", Stolypin changed the Duma's already lopsided election process, dropping the value of a worker's vote by one third and a peasant's vote by half. With the peasantry and the proletariat effectively eliminated, the Third Duma was dominated by the Russian bourgeoisie.

As the decade went on, however, the Duma's power began to increase. When World War I broke out in 1914, the Russian merchant class, eager for a chance to expand Russian industry into the Balkans, pushed for expansionism. Prodded by the Russian merchant class and manipulated by the French and British who controlled the economy, Russia's entry into the war was inevitable. On August 6,1914, Austria-Hungary declared war on Russia, and the unprepared Tsarist Army found itself at war.

By the time the Germans invaded, the Russian Army could only scrape together enough rifles for half its troops. The Army had only 12% of its required machine guns and 10% of the artillery shells it needed. In a replay of the Russo-Japanese debacle, the Army received one crushing defeat after another.

As the war dragged on and conditions worsened, rebellions flared up. Between 1914 and 1917, the cost of food in the cities went up 566%, while wages rose only 515%. The first major strike broke out on January 9, 1917, when the Petrograd (St Petersburg had been re-named because the old name sounded "too German") printers demonstrated on the anniversary of 1905's Bloody Sunday.

Despite the strike, few thought that, within weeks, Russia would be swept in the flames of revolution. Even Lenin remarked in January 1917, "We, the older generation, perhaps will not live to see the decisive battles of the approaching revolution." When the Duma convened on February 14, 1917, it had no idea that it was about to be engulfed by the February Revolution.

Like the 1905 Revolution before it, the February Revolution began with a general strike. This time, however, no incident or group had called the strike into being. February 23, 1917, was International Women's Day, but no revolutionary group had called for demonstrations that day. Instead, as Trotsky writes, "The overgrown bread lines had provided the last stimulus. . . . A mass of women, not all of them workers, flocked to the Municipal Duma, demanding bread." This demonstration quickly spread into a general strike, which immediately took on a political character. Trotsky recalled, "Red banners appeared in different parts of the city, and the inscriptions on them showed that the workers wanted bread, but neither autocracy nor war."

This time, however, the revolutionaries realized that a general strike alone would not accomplish what needed to be done — the overthrow of Tsarism. If the insurrection were begun, it must be carried through to its completion. Significantly, the power of the Duma had been so weakened that nobody looked to it for leadership. The bourgeoisie who would soon inherit power through the Revolution did little to bring it about. Rather, says Trotsky, "The gigantic tasks thus presented to the proletariat gave rise to an urgent necessity for a special revolutionary organization capable of quickly getting hold of the popular masses and making them ready for revolutionary action under the leadership of the workers. Thus, the soviets of 1905 developed gigantically in 1917."

When the Third Duma was dissolved on February 26, its deputies could not even defy the Tsar's decree. Instead of rising immediately to lead the Revolution, the Duma disbanded, its sharpest act of rebellion being its decision that the delegates would remain in Petrograd.

To the Russian feudal nobility, it was becoming obvious that the autocracy was fighting for its life. To the bourgeoisie, it was as obvious that the revolutionaries intended to destroy it along with the aristocracy, and the merchant class was unable to stop them. Thus, the Russian bourgeoisie hung in limbo; unable to lead the Revolution to victory, it was likewise unable to prevent the Revolution from destroying it.

In desperation, the Russian merchant class tried to bargain for its life, working with Tsarist officials to somehow control the revolutionary movement that was sweeping through the streets of Petrograd. At one point, Duma officials suggested to Grand Duke

Mikhail that he take control and ask the Tsar to grant responsibility to the Duma to form a Cabinet and end the rebellion.

But it was already too late for the Russian bourgeoisie. On February 27, the day on which the Duma formed its Provisional Committee, the Tsarist Army began to take its weapons and join the ranks of the revolutionaries. The formation of the Petrograd Soviet of Worker's Delegates signaled the end of the bourgeoisie's dreams of domination.

On February 28, the Tsarist Ministers were placed under arrest. On March 2, Tsar Nicholas II formally abdicated, leaving Grand Duke Mikhail as head of government. On the same day, the Duma formed its first Provisional Government, dominated by the Kadets. On March 3, Grand Duke Mikhail himself abdicated. The Duma's Provisional Government, though weak and inadequate, remained as the only central power in Russia. The Russian merchant class's dream had at last come true; it stood at the head of a republican government.

If the Duma had done virtually nothing to bring about the Revolution which toppled the Tsar and brought it to power, neither had the revolutionary parties. As Milovan Djilas points out;

> Communist historians . . . describe the revolution as if it were the fruit of the previously planned action of its leaders. But only the course of the revolution and the armed struggle was consciously planned, while the forms which the revolution took stemmed from the immediate course of events and from the direct action taken.

John Reed would later declare, "It was the masses of people, workers, soldiers and peasants, which forced every change in the course of the revolution." In fact, notes Trotsky, many of the radical organizations had attempted to end the general strike, saying that it was too early to start the insurrection. "Thus," writes

Trotsky, "the fact is that the Revolution was begun from below, overcoming the resistance of its own revolutionary organizations, the initiative being taken of their own accord by the most oppressed and downtrodden part of the proletariat — the women textile workers, among them no doubt many worker's wives."

It was this lack of leadership, the absence of any central authority able to rally around itself the population of the entire country, that enabled the delegates of the Duma to keep power for eight months. While each major city had its Soviet, and many peasant Soviets had sprung up in the countryside, each of these was able to control only a limited area. In addition, the Army, which constituted the real power after February, remained for the most part loyal to the new Provisional Government.

Even as the Provisional Government consolidated its position, however, the forces that would kill it were already gathering. On March 29, the first All-Russian Conference of Soviets met in Petrograd, and the Peasant Soviets held a similar congress on May 1. Both the Soviets and the Peasant Councils were dominated by the Mensheviks, who favored stopping the insurrection after bourgeois democracy had been established.

Meanwhile, the Provisional Government was being forced into a fatal move. After the revolution, the Russian people, tired of the war and the hardships it had brought, clamored for peace with Germany. Divisions at the front regularly sent troop delegates to Petrograd to ask for an end to the war. The people, having disposed of the Tsar, now wanted only peace.

Once again, the Russian merchant class found itself to be at odds with the rest of the country. Ending the war, to the bourgeoisie, meant breaking the ties with Britain and France upon which the Russian merchants depended for their survival. The deputies of the Provisional Government had no choice but to continue the war.

The announcement on April 18 by Foreign Minister Miliukov sparked riots and armed demonstrations, known as the "April Days". Miliukov resigned on May 2 and a new Kadet coalition was formed three days later, but the damage had already been done. The unrest over the continuation of the war had added fuel to the fires that had already broken out once again among the peasantry.

In March, the Provisional Government had attempted to increase grain production by declaring the grain trade to be a state monopoly. This provision was only half-heartedly enforced, but the peasants were angered by government controls over pricing, and responded with strikes and riots.

To combat the problem, the Provisional Government set up a Chief Economic Committee to do something about the agrarian problem. The Committee in turn formed a number of Land Committees to "prepare the way for land reform", but the CEC and the Land Committees were controlled by the Russian industrialists and did nothing to improve the lot of the muzhik. As the economic situation worsened, the peasants, supported by the Soviets and several renegade Land Committees, took to burning manor houses and seizing land.

During this time, the Soviets, now dominated by the Bolsheviks, grew in power. Throughout June and July, the Soviets had become de facto local governments, forcibly removing or arresting unpopular foremen and factory owners. The Petrograd Soviet had become powerful enough to demand and get an eight-hour working day. When the Moscow industrialists refused the same demand, the Moscow Soviet enforced the eight-hour day itself, without authorization from the Provisional Government. The Conference of Industrialization bitterly complained to the Ministry of Labor that "criminal elements are going entirely unpunished."

By July 3, the Soviets were strong enough to make a direct bid to overthrow the Provisional Government. The three day street battle, known as the "July Days", failed to topple the government, but demonstrated the growing power of the Soviets. Shaken by the agrarian revolts and the coup attempt, Prince Lvov resigned as head of government, and on July 7 a Socialist government was formed by the Trudoviks under Kerensky. Kerensky announced that he would "abandon completely the old land policy which ruined and demoralized the peasantry", and would act instead according to the principle that "the land is to pass into the hands of those who work it". Nevertheless, Kerensky had no apparatus left to put this program into effect; the Land Committees were powerless and the Bolshevik-dominated Soviets virtually ran the countryside. Unrest and violence continued.

By July 21, Kerensky's authority had deteriorated to the point that he was forced to form a coalition with the Kadets to replace the Socialist government. The unrest continued, and was fueled by Kerensky's step on August 26 of doubling the price of grain in the cities.

Kerensky's government was, however, strong enough to deal a fatal blow to the forces of reaction. On August 27, 1917, General Kornilov began to march his troops on Petrograd, intending to overthrow Kerensky and install himself as the new Tsar. While the Army was dissatisfied with the Kerensky government, they did not want another autocrat. Kornilov's forces, weakened by mass desertions, were crushed within four days, and Kornilov himself was arrested.

Kerensky formed another coalition government on September 24, but it was already hopeless. The Russian bourgeoisie had finally lost the confidence of the Army, which was made up largely of conscripts who had been drafted for the war. Now, the peasants in uniform, like the peasants in the countryside, had tired of the weakness of the coalition government. The troops wanted to end the war, go home and institute a redistribution of land.

With the weakness of the Provisional government, it only remained for another political group to sweep it out of the way and assume power for itself. As Trotsky writes:

> The historic preparation of a revolution brings about, in the pre-revolutionary period, a situation in which the class which is called upon to realize the new social system, although not yet

master of the country, has already actually concentrated in its hands a significant share of the state power, while the official apparatus of the government is still in the hands of the old lords.

Trotsky referred to this alternative power structure as a "dual power".

Such an organization existed in Russia in 1917, in the form of the Soviets. By October 1917, the Bolshevik-led Soviets had concentrated virtual de facto control of the country into their hands. When the Petrograd Soviet called for an All-Russian Soviet Congress to be held on October 20, it was already laying plans to seize power from the Provisional Government and transfer it to the Congress. When the planned coup was delayed, the Congress was pushed back to October 25.

On the appointed day, the Bolsheviks, acting on behalf of the Soviets, seized virtually all of Petrograd without firing a shot. With the arrest the following morning of the Provisional Government, the rule of the Russian merchant class came to an end.

The history of the Russian Revolution duplicates the development of feudalist Europe, up to and including the February Revolution. But, after the establishment of the Kadet government, the Russian Revolution took a direction that no social movement had before. The Bolsheviks introduced a social and economic order that had been previously unknown. In order to understand the direction taken by the Revolution, as well as the direction it would take in the future, we must understand the historical and economic factors which allowed it—even compelled it—to make its appearance.

The key to understanding the process of Leninist revolution is to appreciate the significance of the fact that most of the nation's economic resources were foreign-owned. These foreign financial interests played an active role in Russia's internal development. They dominated and controlled the Russian economy, and stifled and weakened the Russian merchant class. The flow of wealth from Russia to the Western economic powers crippled the Russian economy, making the development of higher productivity and industrial capacity impossible. As a result, Russia became increasingly unable to provide for the needs of its own population. The same process can be seen in any nation that has undergone a Leninist revolution.

If these dominated "neo-colonies" were ever to throw off the foreign financial chains and industrialize themselves, the power of the feudal state and the grip of the foreign imperialists must be broken by a social upheaval—by a revolution. Since the existing state in the neo-colony was feudal in nature, the segment of the population that could carry out this revolution had to be anti-feudal in its outlooks. And, since the grip of the foreign financial powers had to be broken, this segment had to be anti-imperialist and nationalist.

Furthermore, since economic development through the capitalist marketplace had failed to provide growth for the Russian economy, and in fact had hampered Russian development by allowing the penetration of foreign capital, this anti-imperialist and anti-feudal revolutionary movement also had to have an anti-capitalist outlook. Rather than continuing to depend on the capitalist marketplace for new economic growth, this revolutionary segment had to advocate the nationalization of all economic resources, to prevent the flow of wealth out of the country and to utilize those resources in a pre-planned manner to produce the swiftest possible industrialization and economic growth. As Milovan Djilas points out;

> The revolutionary party could not seriously contemplate execution of an industrial revolution unless it concentrated all domestic resources into its own hands, particularly those of the native capitalists, against whom the masses were already embittered because of severe exploitation and the use of inhumane methods. The revolutionary party had to take a similar stand against foreign capital.

In all of the Leninist countries, says Djilas, the Communists alone advocated such a social and economic program;

> Only the Communist Parties were both revolutionary in their opposition to the status quo and staunch and consistent in their support of the industrial transformation. In practice, this meant a radical destruction of established ownership relations. No other party went so far in this respect. None was "industrial" to that degree.

In the context of Russian history, only the Bolsheviks, of all the Russian Marxist revolutionary groups, were able to accomplish the October Revolution. This success was due to the philosophical and organizational system that became known as "Leninism".

Even before the 1905 Revolution, the Marxist parties in Russia realized that, according to the Marxian conception of social development, the coming revolution must be a bourgeois one, that would sweep away feudalism and introduce the capitalist republic. As late as 1903, Axelrod, representing the Mensheviks, declared, "The social relations of Russia have ripened only for a bourgeois revolution."

Lenin, however, refused to accept that assessment, and proposed moving directly from feudalism to socialism. "Bolshevism," writes Trotsky, "refused to acknowledge that the Russian bourgeoisie was capable of consummating its own revolution. To the Plekhanovite idea of union between the proletariat and the liberal bourgeoisie, Lenin counterpoised the idea of union between the proletariat and the peasantry." Trotsky continued:

> In a revolution, the only party that can win the support of the peasantry is the party that leads the most revolutionary masses of the city and does not hesitate to assault feudal property because it is afraid of the property-owning bourgeoisie. Only the Social Democracy is such a party today.

By thus excluding the Russian bourgeoisie from its revolutionary program, the Bolsheviks remained unscathed when the merchant class proved itself to be politically impotent and subsequently collapsed. While both the Kadets and the Mensheviks banked on the bourgeois revolution and failed, Lenin banked on the workers and the peasantry.

Other parties, including the Social Revolutionaries and the Trudoviks, also condemned the bourgeoisie, but put all of their energies into the muzhiks, and ignored the urban working class. To Lenin, it was obvious that the peasantry could not accomplish an industrial revolution on its own, and that the answer lay in a union of the rural muzhik with the industrial worker.

The Leninists built such an alliance, and placed it under the leadership of the petty bourgeois class of intellectuals and managers which alone would be capable of leading an anti-feudal industrial revolution in the absence of a developed bourgeois class. Thus, of all the major parties in Russia in 1917, only the Bolsheviks presented the program that could fulfill the historical and economic obligations of the Revolution and appealed to the sectors of the social structure that could carry this program out.

Indeed, after the collapse of the Russian bourgeoisie in October 1917, the Bolsheviks were the only major party to have any sort of program left. As John Reed notes, "Instead of being a destructive force, it seems to me that the Bolsheviks were the only party in Russia with a constructive program and the power to impose it on the country." Sukhanov, of the Mensheviks, scoffed, "Their 'Bolshevism' was nothing more than hatred for the coalition and longing for land and peace." Indeed, Lenin's slogan of "Bread, Land and Peace" reflected precisely what the Russian people wanted and what the Bolsheviks alone had the power to provide.

Lenin had no doubt that the peasantry would rally to his "Dictatorship of the Proletariat". He once shot back to a doubter, "The dictatorship would give land to the peasants and all power to the peasant Soviets in the localities. How can you in your right mind doubt that the peasantry would support the dictatorship?"

Lenin apparently never considered what effect his reliance on the muzhik would have on his "proletarian" revolution. "Lenin," notes Trotsky, "regarded the peasantry as a petty bourgeois class and the peasant land program as the program of bourgeois progressivism." Lenin's idealist dream of a socialist revolution prevented him from seeing the true nature of his revolution. What he claimed to be the dictatorship of the proletariat was in fact the dictatorship of the urban petty bourgeoisie, aided by the peasantry and the working class. This unique combination now faced the awesome tasks of achieving the rapid industrial revolution that the economy of Russia demanded.

None of this mattered to Lenin. He stood at the head of a successful revolution. Now, he braced himself for the reaction.

THREE : The Soviet Government (1917 to 1925)

When the Second All-Russian Congress of Soviets met in Petrograd on October 25, 1917, it found itself presented with a fait accompli — a Bolshevik coup d'etat that had seized power from the Provisional Government of Kerensky and had transferred it to the Soviets. The Congress of Soviets, Lenin declared, would henceforth govern Russia.

In reality, Lenin's Bolsheviks (now re-named the Communist Party) retained control of the government. When Lenin announced the composition of the Council of People's Commissars, it was no accident that all of the major Commissariats were occupied by Bolsheviks, and Lenin himself served as Chairman. Although Lenin declared that the Council (known as Sovnarkom) was responsible to and could be replaced by the Executive Committee of the Congress of Soviets, his position as both Chairman of Sovnarkom and Chairman of the Communist Party concentrated all of Russia's political power solely in Lenin's hands.

Lenin lost no time in capitalizing on his position to entrench the Communist Party firmly in power. He announced that the Sovnarkom would be given the power to make and enforce legislation, despite the fact that the Congress of Soviets had intended to reserve this power for an elected Constituent Assembly. This further alienated the other opposition parties, who were already angered by the Bolshevik coup. Many socialists, including the Bolsheviks Kamenev and Zinoviev, resigned from the Soviet government to protest the Bolshevik domination.

Lenin defended his actions, arguing that the Revolution could be consolidated "only through dictatorship, because the realization of the transformations immediately and unconditionally necessary for the proletariat and the peasantry will call forth the desperate resistance of the landlords, of the big bourgeoisie, and of Tsarism. Without dictatorship, it would be impossible to defeat counter-revolutionary efforts. That would be, needless to say, not a socialist, but a democratic dictatorship."

After seizing power, however, Lenin promptly forgot about his "democratic dictatorship" and took steps to insure that the Communist Party remained as head of the Revolution. One of the Bolshevik Government's first moves was to create the Chrezvychainya Kommissia ("Committee to Combat Espionage"), better known by the Russian abbreviation "Cheka". While Cheka's original purpose was to control common criminals, it soon turned to arresting "enemies of the people" and other "counter-revolutionaries".

In January 1918, the Sovnarkom received its first serious challenge for power. In the general elections for the Constituent Assembly held by the Congress of Soviets, the Communist Party received only 9 million votes, while the Social Revolutionaries received 16.5 million. When it convened on January 18, the Constituent Assembly elected a Social Revolutionary as its

President, introduced new land reforms and agreed to continue the peace negotiations with Germany opened by Trotsky in August 1917.

The next day, the Constituent Assembly was surrounded by Bolshevik troops and disbanded for serving as "a cover for the struggle of the bourgeois counter-revolution for the overthrow of the Soviets." Since the All-Russian Congress of Soviets had adjourned at about the same time, this action left Sovnarkom as the only central body in Russia, and left the Communists firmly in control.

Whatever Lenin's socialist dreams might have been, however, the rise to power of the Bolsheviks left the petty bourgeois intelligentsia at the helm of state. Despite this, Lenin now made every effort to mold the Russian social system to the goals of socialism. As author Bertram Wolfe notes, "The Marxist view that 'in the last analysis economics determines politics' became the Leninist view that, with enough determination, power itself, naked political power, might succeed wholly in determining economics."

Lenin moved quickly to construct his "socialist system". Just two days after the coup, the Communist Party declared:

> The landowner's right to possession of the land is herewith abolished without compensation. Estates of the landowners, together with all crown lands, monastic lands and church lands, including all livestock and agricultural equipment and farm buildings, are transferred to the disposition of the district Land Committees and the local Soviets of Peasant's Deputies.

The Bolsheviks also continued Kerensky's policy of maintaining a state monopoly on the grain trade, and strengthened this by nationalizing the grain elevators and warehouses.

At first, Sovnarkom only nationalized the heavy industry it needed to consolidate its power. Local Soviets were forbidden from allowing workers to "take possession of the enterprise or direct it" unless one of three conditions applied; (1) the enterprise was of particular importance to the state, (2) the owner of the enterprise refused to follow Sovnarkom or Soviet decrees, or (3) the enterprise had been closed or abandoned by its owner. Sovnarkom established a Supreme Economic Council ("Vesenkha") to oversee the economy.

Within a short time, however, this policy had completely broken down. The Bolsheviks, in essence, sought to maintain the capitalist factory system, and intended merely to substitute the Soviet Government for the owners of the factories. The Russian industrial workers, however, had fought for direct worker control, without the subordination of the workers to any bosses, be they capitalist owners or Party Commissars. Syndicalist workers and renegade Soviets began to expropriate the factories and run them themselves through elected factory councils. The Donetz metal workers, for instance, began to produce and sell iron products directly to the peasantry, ignoring the protests of Vesenkha and the Bolsheviks. Decrees of February 11 and April 27 banning the confiscation of any property without the permission of Vesenkha were ignored by the workers. Of the 500 enterprises that had been seized from their owners in July 1918, only 100 had been taken with the permission of Vesenkha or the Soviets.

This worker's movement towards self-managed socialism presented a grave danger to Bolshevik control over the economy, and Lenin venomously attacked the worker's councils, calling them "anarchist" and "criminal". To keep control, Lenin began to nationalize entire industries and forcibly replaced the elected worker's councils with state-appointed managers. In May, the entire sugar industry was placed under the control of a Supreme Sugar Committee, and in June the entire oil industry was nationalized. The Decree of General Nationalization was made on June 28, 1918, and made all enterprises with capital of over one million rubles state property. By 1919, some 3,000 firms had been nationalized.

Industries which were owned or controlled by foreign capital were taken over by joint stock companies made up of the former owners and the Soviet government. The Centro-Textil, set up in April, was run by a board of thirty representatives from the Soviet trade unions, fifteen foreign stockholders and twenty officials from Vesenkha and the Soviets. Because the trade unions were virtual extensions of the Soviet state, this arrangement guaranteed Communist control over the enterprise.

Despite the nationalization process, however, industrial workers continued to seize their factories and run them themselves. The railroad workers, for instance, seized the railroad lines, formed an Alliance of Worker's Representatives to run them and announced the "autonomy of the worker's committees".

Lenin responded by tightening government control over the industry and by tying railroad workers' wages to their output. In essence, the Bolsheviks were being forced to defend their interests against the very workers in whose name they had seized power. The Social Revolutionaries and the Right Wing of the Social Democrats, which had largely supported the worker's councils, protested against Lenin's "relics of capitalist exploitation" and tried to arrest him on July 6. Later that month, Uritsky, the head of the Petrograd Cheka, was shot by a student, and Lenin himself was shot and wounded by Fanny Kaplan, a Social Revolutionary who wanted to depose the Bolsheviks and return power to the worker's councils.

By August 1918, the split over the worker's councils had reached the point of armed conflict, when groups of Ukrainian insurgents led by Nestor Makhno waged guerrilla warfare to defend their autonomous worker's committees. The Makhnovites at one point controlled a huge area of the Ukraine, and carried on their guerrilla fight for several years. The rift between the Bolsheviks and the Social Revolutionaries grew, leading to armed conflict and civil war. Other political groups chose sides, and soon the Bolsheviks and the Left Social Revolutionaries stood against the "White Russians", a loose conglomeration of Social Revolutionaries, Mensheviks and former Tsarist officials.

In the summer of 1918, after the Soviet Government announced that the foreign debt compiled by the Tsar would not be repaid, the White Russians were joined by a group of British Royal Marines. Within a short time, Japan, France, Canada and the United States had all sent combat troops to join the Whites. Other countries aided the Whites with military and economic aid.

By this time, Lenin was also having trouble with nationalist groups in Georgia, the Ukraine, Lithuania and other non-Russian areas. After the October Revolution, the Georgian Mensheviks had set up a republic with Noah Zhordania as Premiere. In May 1920, the Bolsheviks concluded a treaty recognizing the legitimacy of the Zhordania government. In February 1921, however, the Red Army moved into Georgia, deposed the republic and imposed Soviet rule. Georgian nationalists carried out guerrilla warfare against the occupiers, culminating in another failed uprising in 1921.

Lenin, hoping to end the Civil War quickly, told a US diplomat, in Russia on a fact-finding tour in March 1919, that he was willing to allow "all existing de facto governments which have been set up on the territory of the former Russian Empire and Finland to remain in full control of the territories which they occupy at the moment when the armistice becomes effective." This, in fact, amounted to almost three-fourths of Russia, which was either in White hands or had declared its national independence. The US failed to act on the offer.

In addition to political problems, the Civil War produced crushing economic problems for the Soviet Government. Almost all of the nation's coal reserves were lost to Soviet control, and less than one-fourth of the nation's iron foundries remained in Soviet hands. The production of steel fell from 4.2 million tons to 183,000 tons, while the grain harvest fell from 801 million hundredweight to 503 million.

The peasantry in particular were hard hit by the Civil War. Inflation drove the prices of manufactured goods up, while the government monopoly kept grain prices low. The Soviets, in turn, aggravated the situation by paying for their grain purchases by simply printing more money, thus driving inflation even higher.

Faced with rapid price increases, the muzhiks, who up to now had been hoarding money in order to buy manufactured goods, now scrambled to buy them quickly before the next price increase. The resulting run on manufactured goods drove prices even higher.

As the Civil War dragged on, the grain situation became more and more desperate. The government needed grain to feed its Red Army and its industrial workers, and also needed agrarian reserves to sell abroad for badly needed investment funds. At the same time, however, the Soviets were unable to produce the manufactured goods for which the muzhiks exchanged their grain.

To combat the problem, the Soviets introduced a series of measures under the name "War Communism". To extract as much value as possible from the peasantry, the Soviets set the prices of manufactured goods high, forcing the peasantry to pay more for them than they were worth. Predictably, the muzhiks responded by simply holding their grain, rather than trading it for inflated prices. In desperation, many Soviets set up "Committees of the Village Poor" to forcibly seize any surplus grain being withheld by the peasantry. Since the Committees were often quite arbitrary in their definition of "surplus" supplies, this system of confiscation greatly antagonized the muzhiks. The Bolsheviks had to intervene to make the confiscations less heavy-handed. They also talked about setting a minimum area to be sown by each farm, but never put this plan into effect.

Russian industry, meanwhile, was not faring much better. In November 1920, the Soviets attempted to increase industrial production by nationalizing all firms with five or more employees using mechanical power or ten or more employees without machinery. Each area of the economy was assigned to an industrial department of Vesenkha known as Glavki.

The system broke down almost immediately. Most of the country's engineers had fled or didn't support the Bolsheviks in the first place. The Glavki themselves were often out of touch with the industry they were supposed to be overseeing. At the 9th Communist Party Congress in 1920, the Glavki system was criticized as being too bureaucratic and unwieldy. Consequently, at the Congress of Soviets in December 1920, the number of Glavki was cut from 52 to 16, with some 2,000 enterprises being placed under local Soviet control.

By 1921, it was apparent that the policies of "War Communism" were inadequate. Lenin, in 1921, explained its shortcomings by noting, "War Communism was thrust upon us by war and ruin. It was not, nor could it be, a policy that corresponded to the economic tasks of the proletariat. It was a temporary measure." Trotsky echoed, "War Communism was, in fact, the systematic regimentation of consumption in a besieged fortress."

Trotsky, however, apparently had higher goals for the system than had Lenin. He writes, "It is necessary to acknowledge, however, that in its original conception it pursued broader aims. The Soviet Government hoped and strove to develop these methods of regimentation directly into a system of planned economy in distribution as well as production. In other words, from 'War Communism' it hoped gradually, but without destroying the system, to arrive at genuine communism."

The economic problems of 1918 to 1921, however, convinced the Bolsheviks that the policies of War Communism could not be permanent. Trotsky recalls, "Reality, however, came into increasing conflict with the program of 'War Communism'."

The basic problem faced by the Soviets in 1921 was how to obtain the funds and resources needed for a rapid expansion of the industrial sector. The hostility of the Western powers made it impossible to borrow or import capital, leaving the Bolsheviks with no choice but to extract this capital from some internal source. Under War Communism, high prices on industrial goods forced the peasantry to transfer wealth to the government, thus providing a source of surplus for investment.

However, the peasantry responded by withholding their stocks of grain, aggravating the country's economic problems. In March 1921, the Kronstadt sailors mutinied to protest rising food prices, and further demanded an end to the Bolshevik regime and the transfer of power to elected worker councils. The revolt was crushed by the Red Army, but the lesson was not lost on Lenin. He wearily told the 10th Party Congress, "We do not need any opposition now, Comrades, it is not the time for it. . . . And, in my view, the Congress will have to draw the conclusion that the time has come to put an end to opposition, to put the lid on it. We have had enough opposition." The Party Congress responded by placing a "temporary ban" on all opposing factions within the Party.

To improve Russia's economy and prevent further outbreaks, Lenin announced the end of "War Communism" and the relaxation of economic controls under a New Economic Policy. Lenin proposed to loosen the Glavki system, which had proven to be ineffective and cumbersome. "Borne along on the crest of a wave of enthusiasm," he remarked, "we reckoned . . . on being able to organize the state production and the state distribution of products on a communist line in a small peasant country by order of the proletarian state. Experience has proved that we were wrong."

Thus, Lenin was forced to admit that the use of political or military force can do nothing to change socio-economic realities. If Russia was to become industrialized, this industrialization must be undertaken by the state: "We must first set to work in this small peasant country to build solid little gangways to socialism by way of state capitalism, otherwise we will never get to communism." At the time, Lenin had no idea what his "state capitalism" would lead to.

The New Economic Policy began the process of dismantling the old system of War Communism and introduced a new method for the state to extract investible capital from the muzhik. Instead of setting industrial prices high by government fiat, the Soviets would now allow agrarian prices to rise under the influence of the marketplace, thus, it was hoped, providing an incentive for the peasantry to produce more agricultural materials. Under NEP, the muzhik was given a set quota which would be provided to the state as a tax, and the state would pay higher prices for any production over quota. The state monopoly on grain trade was ended, and private traders, known as NEPmen, were allowed to trade factory goods for grain. After a time, the quota set for the state was replaced with a monetary tax.

Lenin explained his new program: "We are still in a state of ruin, so crushed by the burden of war . . . that we cannot give the peasant manufactured goods for all the grain we require. Knowing this, we are introducing the food tax, i.e.. we shall take the minimum of grain we require (for the army and the workers) in the form of a tax and will obtain the rest in exchange for manufactured goods."

In October 1922, Bukharin proposed lifting the state monopoly on foreign trade and allowing individual Russians to trade with foreigners. This, argued Bukharin, would boost Russia's sagging foreign exchange and would provide a supply of badly needed investment capital. In December, however, Trotsky pointed out that individual foreign trade was resulting in the flow of Russia's scarce resources to the West, and had the government monopoly restored.

By this time, however, the problems of Russian industry had little to do with foreigners. The urban factories, short on food and agrarian raw materials, were anxious to begin trading manufactured products to the muzhiks. The 1921 famine, however, had left the peasantry with little to sell, and agricultural prices soared over manufactured prices. Lenin, realizing that the entire Russian economy was tottering, declared, "The salvation of Russia lies not only in a good harvest on the peasant farms, that is not enough; and not only in the good condition of light industry which provides the peasantry with consumer goods—this too is not enough; we also need heavy industry. . . . Unless we save heavy industry, unless we restore it, we shall not be able to build any industry—we shall be doomed as an independent country."

While industrial output continued to fall, rising administrative costs from the bloated Glavki bureaucracy pushed the prices of manufactured goods up. By 1923, the situation of

1921 had been reversed; now industrial prices were over three times higher than the cost of agricultural products.

If the Russian economy were to be stabilized, the output of Russian industry had to be increased sharply. In 1921, industrial output was only 18% of its 1916 level. By 1922, it was only 27% of pre-war levels, and by 1923 had risen to only 35%. By contrast, the area of land under cultivation was, in 1923, up to 80% of the 1916 level, and grain production was up to 70% of pre-war levels.

In 1925, the Soviets legalized the use of hired labor in agriculture and permitted the rental of land. This policy led to the rapid growth of the kulaks, who rented land, horses and machinery to those peasants who couldn't afford to buy them. In addition, the kulaks often bought grain from the muzhiks at low prices during the harvest, when taxes were due and the peasants needed the cash, and later sold the same grain back to the muzhiks at prices 30 to 50% higher.

Nevertheless, the kulaks led the growth of Russian agriculture after the Civil War. The kulaks produced only 35% of the total grain output, but sold nearly all of it, while the muzhiks sold only 25% of their crops and consumed the rest. Kulak farms produced only one-eighth of the nation's wheat crop, but sold nearly half of all the marketed supplies, providing badly-needed foreign exchange.

By 1925, it was apparent that the New Economic Policy was unable to produce the rapid industrialization that was needed. The NEP, it was apparent, was simply too favorable to the agrarian kulaks, and left the Soviets with no way of tapping into this wealth for investment in industrial production. As Trotsky pointed out, "The peasantry was becoming polarized between the small capitalist on the one side and the hired hand on the other. At the same time, lacking industrial commodities, the state was crowded out of the rural markets."

Trotsky concluded, "The rising tide of capitalism was everywhere."

FOUR: Collectivization and Industrialization (1925 to 1953)

The conflicts between the agrarian and the industrial sectors that took place in the Soviet Union in the 1920's had also occurred in the development of Western Europe. Realizing that the individual production developed under feudalism could not produce industrial gains, the European bourgeoisie, after seizing power, began the development of the factory system, in which labor was divided into a number of tasks performed by separate workers, thus increasing output and productivity. As Engels writes:

> The peasant sold to the artisan agricultural products, and bought from him the products of handicraft. Into this society of individual producers, of commodity producers, the new mode of production thrust itself. In the midst of the old division of labor, grown up spontaneously and upon no definite plan,

which had governed the whole of society, now arose division of labor upon a definite plan, as organized in the factory; side by side with individual production appeared social production. The products of both were sold in the same market and, therefore, at prices approximately equal. But organization upon a definite plan was stronger than spontaneous division of labor. The factories, working with the combined social forces of a collectivity of individuals, produced their commodities far more cheaply than the individual small producers. Individual production succumbed in one department after another. Socialized production revolutionized all the old methods of production.

Engels added,

But the bourgeoisie . . . could not transform these puny means of production into mighty productive forces without transforming them, at the same time, from means of production of the individual into the social means of production only workable by a collectivity of men.

By 1925, the Soviet Union found itself in a similar position. The Russian petty bourgeois ruling party, faced with the urgent need to increase industrial output as rapidly as possible, found the factory system of the bourgeoisie, under private ownership, to be inadequate for this task. Unable to depend solely on the factory system to increase industrialization, as the European bourgeoisie had done, the Soviet Union was forced to turn to an even more radical "division of labor upon a definite plan". While the planned economy had long been a cornerstone of socialist and communist thought, the Leninists now used it as a tool to suit their own class interests.

In December 1929, Ossinsky advocated a solution to the industrialization problem by submitting a resolution to the Moscow Party Groups, pointing out that economic problems were worsening because of "the lack of a plan uniting the work of all the branches of the state economy." Arguing that "the attempt, instead of aiming at a general economic plan, to regulate the economy from its financial center" was bound to fail, Ossinsky proposed that a plan for rapid industrialization be drawn up and administered by a State Planning Commission ("Gosplan").

Ossinsky's ideas were supported by Trotsky, who asserted, "In the struggle of state industry for conquest of the market, the plan is our principle weapon. . . Gosplan should control all the fundamental factors of state economy, to coordinate them with one another and with the peasant economy. Its central work should be to develop state industry."

Supporters of a centrally-planned economy pointed out that progress through capitalist supply and demand was far too slow for the rapid industrialization that the Soviet economy needed. Emphasis on yield, it was argued, produced much swifter gain than emphasis on profitability.

In addition, it was argued, under a market economy, people would be naturally more willing to pay for consumer goods than for heavy industrial investment. If Soviet heavy industry were to be rapidly expanded, central price setting would be necessary to keep the prices of consumer goods high and thus discourage their use and allow more resources to flow into the industrialization effort.

Finally, it was noted, opening the Soviet economy to market investment would, in the absence of government controls, result in a flood of foreign capital. This foreign capital would crush indigenous investments and dominate the economy, in essence returning the Soviet Union to its pre-1917 condition as a neo-colony.

The argument over central planning was symptomatic of a struggle which had broken out within the Communist Party. By 1925, Stalin's faction had established itself as dominant. Stalin tended to favor the agrarian sector and the muzhiks in his economic policies, and argued in favor of providing land to the peasantry so that small individual farms could be built. He was opposed by the Right Opposition, which tended to favor a type of "market socialism" in which state-owned industry competed with small private producers. The Left Opposition argued in favor of a centrally planned state-owned economy.

In 1923, the Left Opposition, led by Trotsky, had first introduced the idea of a centralized plan, combined with an increase in hydroelectric dams and other industrial projects. The idea was ridiculed by the Stalin faction, which argued in favor of forming small peasant farms and postponing industrialization for a time.

The Trotsky faction responded by arguing that industrialization was vital, and that the peasantry had to serve as the source of labor and capital for industrial investment. As Preobrazhensky pointed out, in the absence of any foreign sources of capital, the Soviet Union could only increase capital investment in one of two ways: (1) it could generate a surplus by producing manufactured goods that were worth more than their cost of production, or (2) it could coerce the consumer into paying more for goods than they were worth. With the weakness of Soviet industry, Preobrazhensky concluded, the first alternative could be ruled out.

Realizing the implications of Preobrazhensky's conclusions, Rykov, of the Right Opposition, shot back, "Every kopeck which can be supplied for the reconstruction of industry must be expended for this purpose without the slightest delay. But this must be done by forming an alliance with the peasantry, and not by fixing prices which the peasantry could not possibly pay." The 13th Party Congress in 1921 sided with the Right, and declared that exchange between the cities and the countryside was to be encouraged by lowering the price of manufactured goods.

This declaration did little to increase industrial output. By 1925, writes Trotsky, it had become obvious that "for any further advance industrial construction on a large scale was necessary. It was impossible to lead any further gropingly and without a plan."

By 1928, Stalin realized that the Soviet Union could not survive economically without a greatly expanded productive ability, and that industrial development was vital. "We are fifty to a hundred years behind the advanced countries," he concluded. "We must make good this lag in ten years. Either we do it or we go under." The First Five Year Plan adopted in 1929 was almost an exact duplicate of that put forward by the Left Opposition in 1923.

Thus, the Soviet economy was planned solely for the production of heavy industry as rapidly as possible. Inevitably, this produced problems. As economist Alec Nove writes, "Soviet policymakers did not seek to adapt themselves to the demand pattern; the point was to change the demand pattern, the institutions, the structure of the economy. The economy was deliberately so organized as to facilitate this drastic and complex process, and this led to the neglect not only of non-priority sectors of economic life, but also of the finer adjustments required for 'optimal' resource allocation."

The Communist Party bureaucrats, however, were not interested in "fine adjustments" or "non-priority sectors". Their sole interest was to increase output as rapidly as possible, whatever the cost. The entire population was harnessed to the task of, as Gosplan put it, transforming the USSR "from a country which imports machines to a country which produces machines, in order that by this means the Soviet Union, in the midst of capitalist encirclement, should not become an appendage of the capitalist world economy, but an independent economic union which is building socialism."

Every available pair of hands was drafted towards fulfilling the Plan. Skilled labor was obtained by offering tuition-free college or technical school in exchange for three years of service in the field. Labor was conscripted from the rural areas and put to work in factories and manufacturing plants.

Nevertheless, the industrialization was being hampered by problems in the agrarian sector. The end of NEP in 1925 had led to the decline of the kulaks, who had been providing most of the marketed grain. The 1926 harvest, while overtaking the pre-war yield, produced only 70% of the pre-war market supplies. Only 17% of the harvest was sold to foreign markets. The Soviets were completely dependent on foreign exchange for their investable surplus, and were likewise dependent on agrarian efficiency both to provide industrial workers and to feed the urban populations. The sluggishness of the Soviet agricultural sector was holding back the Five Year Plan.

To increase agrarian output and combat the problem, the 11th Party Congress ended the restrictions that had been placed on the kulaks and directed the Soviets to use economic incentives to extend cooperation with the agrarian sector. Concessions were also made in the use of hired labor and the renting of land.

The Left Opposition charged that this policy would, in fact, lead to the domination of the villages by the kulaks. At the 15th Party Congress, Trotsky presented figures showing that the kulaks made up only 15-25% of the peasantry, but owned 25-40% of the sown area and 40-60% of all the farm machinery in the USSR. The Congress, while concluding that Trotsky's figures were inaccurate, nevertheless concluded that the kulaks had to be curtailed. A Gosplan report prepared at the time reported that the top 10% of the peasantry held 33% of the sown area, 33% of farm machinery and 40% of the marketable surplus.

The agrarian problem was a crucial one for the Soviet Government. If the USSR wished to remain independent, it had no choice but to industrialize rapidly through the Five Year Plan. But the Plan itself was being jeopardized by the lack of agricultural growth. Economist Maurice Dobb points out, "Progress was occurring, and was likely to continue; but the rate of progress seemed destined to be slow, too slow to increase the yield of agriculture at a speed at all commensurate with the needs of a growing industry. If industry had to march in step with peasant agriculture, no more than a very low rate of industrialization could be placed upon the agenda."

Members of the Right Opposition argued for improving agrarian output by giving the peasantry economic incentives through the marketplace. This was rejected by both the Stalinists and the Left Opposition, who countered that such a policy would lead to the domination of the kulak. Molotov told the Party Congress, "The question is not whether it is necessary or not to make a 'sharper attack' on the kulak. It is obvious that we must, and there is nothing to dispute about it here. What we are concerned with is the best method of conducting this attack."

This decision was, in fact, a major reversal for the Stalinists. In 1925, Stalin had laid plans to de-nationalize the land and talked of putting off industrialization for several years. In July 1928, he had remarked, "There are people who think that individual farms have exhausted their usefulness, that we should not support them. . . . These people have nothing in common with the line of our party." This policy brought support from Rykov, who argued, "To develop individual farms is . . . the chief task of the party."

By the time of the Five Year Plan, however, the Stalinists were forced to recognize that rapid industrialization was vital for the very existence of an independent Soviet economy, and that individual farms would simply not be strong enough to support this effort. To solve the industrialization dilemma, Stalin told the 15th Party Congress, the small farms had to be sacrificed:

> The way out is to turn the small and scattered peasant farms into large united farms based on the common cultivation of the soil, on the basis of new and higher technique. The way out is to unite the small and dwarf peasant farms gradually and surely, not by pressure, but by example and persuasion, into large farms based on common, cooperative use of agricultural machines and tractors and on scientific methods of intensive agriculture. There is no other way out.

These new "collective farms" possessed a number of advantages over individual peasant farms. Small farmers found it difficult to purchase tractors or other machinery, and were thus unable to improve their output by mechanical methods. A large farm, however, would be able to use agrarian machinery and greatly increase the yield per acre. Also, since fewer laborers were needed to run a mechanized farm, the surplus agrarian workers could be transferred to the cities, where they could be put to use in the industrialization effort.

Finally, the collectives solved the Soviet government's problems in extracting surplus wealth from the agrarian sector. Under War Communism, the state attempted to set high prices so that wealth could be transferred from peasant purchasers to the state. Under this system, though, the peasantry was able to withhold supplies rather than trade them for inflated prices. Under the New Economic Policy, the state attempted to use low prices to induce the peasants to produce and trade more, but this arrangement benefited the peasantry more than the state.

The solution adopted by the Stalinists was simple; the peasantry would be organized into collective farms, be provided with machinery and mechanization, and would be compelled to produce a quota that would be forcibly taken from them by the state. By simply removing their ability to resist, the Stalinists were able to avoid the necessity of economic incentives to spur peasant agrarian production.

The First Five Year Plan called for the number of collective farms in the Soviet Union to increase from just 2% of the total to 25%, and from 1% of total cultivated area to 15% by 1933. In practice, this target was greatly exceeded.

When the collectivization program began in 1928, Stalin, in a burst of optimism, declared that the muzhiks were inherently socialistic in their outlooks, and would gladly join the collectives to work towards "socialism in one country". If he sincerely believed that, however, he was in for a rude awakening. The peasantry, instead of welcoming the introduction of state farms (sovkhoz) and collective farms (kolkhoz), resisted them fiercely. Machinery and equipment were smashed, and instructors sent from Moscow were assaulted and harassed. The kulaks, rather than surrendering their grain to the Soviets, burned large areas of crops and slaughtered so many cattle and pigs that the loss was not made up until 1935. Stalin's attempts to "communize" even the muzhik's chickens provoked such widespread opposition that, at the end of 1929, only 3.9% of the USSR's farms had been collectivized, and the major agrarian areas were under virtual military occupation.

To placate the peasantry, Stalin changed the kolkhoz from a "commune" to a collective venture, which allowed each muzhik to own a small private plot of land and livestock in addition to the collective lands. With this concession, collectivization went more smoothly. By 1932, collective and state farms made up 61.5% of all the farms in the USSR.

For this gain, however, Stalin had paid a high price. The bitter fight over collectivization had produced a shortage of agrarian supplies and raw materials, leading to a decline in industrial productivity of 11.7% in 1931. In 1932, industrial production rose only 8.5% instead of the planned 36%. The destruction of food and livestock produced the 1932-1933 famine in which 5 million died.

The Trotskyite faction of the Party bitterly criticized Stalin's heavy-handed methods during the collectivization fiasco. "The blame for these sacrifices," Trotsky wrote, "lies not upon collectivization, but upon the blind, violent, gambling methods by which it was carried through. . . Collectivization could and should have assumed a more reasonable tempo and more deliberate forms. Having in its hands both the power and the industries, the bureaucracy could have regulated the process without carrying the nation to the edge of disaster. They could have, and should have, adopted tempos better corresponding to the material and moral resources of the country."

Trotsky pointed out that Soviet industry was quite unable to support the massive agrarian program put in place by the Stalinists: "The real possibilities of collectivization are determined, not by the depth of the impasse in the villages and not by the administrative energy of the government, but primarily by the existing productive resources — that is, the ability of the industries to furnish large-scale agriculture with the requisite machinery. These material conditions were lacking. The collective farms were set up with an equipment suitable in the main only for small-scale farming."

Despite the inefficiency and the brutality of the collectivization process, it served its purposes. By the 1930's, the collective farms were being instructed to provide quotas of workers for the industrialization effort. These workers were assigned to factory jobs by draft. In 1928, Stalin introduced the labor book, which kept track of an employee's work record. At the same time, it was made illegal for a worker to leave for a new job without giving the employer a month's notice. In 1940, a law was passed preventing any employee from leaving a job without permission from the employer. Increasingly, the worker's employer was the Soviet state itself. Between 1928 and 1937, the state-owned enterprises' share of GNP jumped from 69.4% to 91.8%.

Despite the industrialization efforts, little progress was being made in the Soviet economy. The lack of food and raw materials brought about by the collectivization fiasco slowed industrial development to a crawl. At the same time, increasing opposition to the Stalinists was becoming more bold. *Pravda* attributed the economic problems to a deliberate "economic counter-revolution", blaming it on "capitalist organizations in the West". "We have internal enemies, we have external enemies," *Pravda* warned. "This, comrades, must not be forgotten for a single moment."

By this time, the petty bourgeois managers had set up a complete bureaucracy, guaranteeing them control over the state and the economy. Following Marx's dictum — "The same men who establish their social relations in conformity with their material productivity, produce also principles, ideas and categories, in conformity with their social relationships" — the Soviet ruling bureaucracy produced an ideology and an apparatus designed solely to safeguard its position of economic privilege. Trotsky wrote:

The basis of bureaucratic rule is the poverty of society in the objects of consumption, with the resulting struggle of each against all. When there are enough goods in a store. the purchasers can come whenever they want to. When there are few goods, the purchasers are compelled to stand in line. When the lines are very long, it is necessary to appoint a policeman to keep order. Such is the starting point of the power of the Soviet bureaucracy. It "knows" who is to get something and who has to wait.

Predictably, the lion's share of the goods produced go to the bureaucrats and managers who run the system. The bureaucracy's control over pricing, and the huge salaries and bonuses it grants itself, form the basis for the Communist Party's position of privilege. As Rakovsky complained. "The social situation of the communist who has at his disposal an automobile, a good apartment, regular vacations and receives the party maximum of salary, differs from the situation of the communist who works in the coal mines, where he receives from fifty to sixty rubles a month."

Trotsky concluded, "The Stalinist bureaucracy is nothing else than the first stage of the bourgeois restoration." In this, Trotsky was correct, but in a different way than he imagined. In fact, as Milovan Djilas would later point out, the Soviet bureaucracy was not simply another form of capitalism, but was a "new class", an entirely different form of economic exploitation:

In practice, the ownership privilege of the new class manifests itself as an exclusive right, as a party monopoly, for the political bureaucracy to distribute the national income, to set wages, direct economic development, and dispose of nationalized and other property. . . . It is bureaucracy which formally uses, administers and controls both nationalized and socialized property as well as the entire life of society. The role of the bureaucracy in society, i.e., monopolistic administration and control of national income and national goods, consigns to it a special privileged position. Social relationships resemble state capitalism. . . . Ownership is nothing more than the right of profit and control. If one defines class benefits by this right, the Communist states have seen, in the final analysis, the origin of a new form of ownership or of a new ruling and exploiting class.

This "new form of ownership" was state capitalism or petty bourgeois socialism, and it resulted from the contradictions of a decaying feudal society that lacked a bourgeoisie strong enough to bring about industrialization.

Under these circumstances, socialist revolution is impossible. If an economic neo-colony is to gain its national independence and build an independent economy, it must use the expedients of a state-owned and centrally-planned industrialization program to build up the necessary economic forces. This, in turn, demands the establishment of a centralized, pyramidal state apparatus which oversees and at the same time derives its privileges from this economic structure.

The rigid hierarchical centralization that enabled the Bolsheviks to survive Tsarist repression were simply adapted to the hierarchical government necessary to accelerate the industrialization program. "Stalin," concludes Djilas, "was the lawful, though wicked, offspring of Lenin and the Revolution."

Ironically, it was the same Trotsky who had earlier argued for the destruction of the self-managed workers councils who first spoke out against the increasing centralization of the Soviet government. In 1923, he warned, "There has been created a very broad stratum of Party workers, entering into the administrative apparatus of the Party, who completely renounce their Party opinion, at least the open expression of it, as if assuming that the secretarial hierarchy is the apparatus which creates Party opinion and Party decisions. Beneath this stratum, abstaining from opinion, there lies the broad mass of the Party, before whom every decision stands in the form of a summons or a command."

In January 1925, Trotsky was condemned by the Party for "attempting to bring about a radical change in the Party leadership", i.e., for trying to remove Stalin. By 1927, the Left Opposition leaders Trotsky, Kamenev and Zinoviev were off the Politburo, and Trotsky was exiled in January 1929.

But Trotsky's exile did not end Stalin's campaign. The Left Opposition threatened the stability of the bureaucratic state and, Stalin concluded, had to be eliminated. "It is one thing to arrest Trotskyist cadres and to expel them from the Party," Stalin told the Politburo. "It is another thing to put an end to the Trotskyist ideology. That will be more difficult."

In a massive effort to consolidate his rule, Stalin rounded up thousands of suspected Trotskyites and expelled, imprisoned or exiled them. Krupskaya, Lenin's widow, remarked in disgust, "If Lenin were alive now, he would probably be in one of Stalin's jails."

By 1930, Stalin's power was unchallenged, protected by a pyramidal government that was so corrupt that, as one muzhik remarked. "If they ordered us to elect a horse to the village Soviet, we should be compelled to do so." Alexander Barmine, a Soviet official who defected to the West, remarked that Stalin was widely known as Vozhd, "the Boss". Barmine reported, "Initiative on the part of subordinate bureaucrats is stifled. Everyone seeks to avoid responsibility. Everyone looks to the top for a covering order. And, since thousands of relatively unimportant, as well as the all-important, problems must pass through Stalin's hands for final decision, the top is always jammed."

The collectivization fiasco and continuing industrial stagnation, however, began to bring increasing opposition. In 1932, Ryutin was expelled from the Party for advocating economic self-determination for the muzhik, including the right to leave the kolkhoz. A newly formed Laboring Peasants' Party was crushed, and its leaders were imprisoned or exiled. At the 17th Party Congress, Stalin's own power was reduced, while several of his critics, including Bukharin, Rykov, Tomsky and Kirov, gained key

Party positions. Determined to end the Right Opposition as he had the Left, Stalin had Kirov assassinated in December 1934.

The rise of Hitler and Mussolini in Europe, moreover, forced Stalin to consider these foreign threats as well as his own internal challenges. In the mid-1930's, Stalin took drastic steps to insure that his position of privilege would remain safe.

The first of the "Purge Trials" targeted Left Opposition leaders Zinoviev, Kamenev, and fourteen others. In a public "show trial" that featured coerced confessions and fraudulent evidence, they were charged with various "counter-revolutionary activities". The trial ended on August 23, 1936, and all sixteen defendants were shot later that night. Between 1936 and 1938, half a million of Stalin's opponents were shot, and another seven million were jailed or sent to work camps. Of the 2,000 delegates who had participated in the 17th Party Congress, only 59 were left to participate in the 18th Congress. Fearful that a military coup would remove him from power, Stalin thoroughly purged the Red Army, removing 30,000 senior officers, 90% of the Generals, 75 members of the Supreme Military Council and all 11 Vice Commissars of Defense. This decimation of the Army leadership would have devastating effects during the Second World War.

By this time, it was also apparent that Japan's expansion in the Pacific would mean trouble for the Soviets. Eager to increase industrial output to build war materials, the USSR negotiated a long-term loan of 200 million gold marks with Germany in exchange for guaranteed Soviet purchases of German industrial equipment. Accordingly, the Second Five Year Plan cut provisions for growth in consumer industries in favor of military production.

Between 1938 and 1939, Stalin, fearing a German attack through Poland, tried to negotiate a four-way pact between the USSR, Poland, France and Britain. The proposal failed when Poland and Britain backed out. When Ribbentrop offered a German-Soviet Pact, Stalin jumped at the chance to buy time, saying, "Russian interests come before everything."

Nevertheless, when the Germans invaded in June 1941, the Red Army, weakened by the purges and lacking equipment, was routed. Fearing that the demoralized Army would refuse to fight, Stalin had a Political Commissar attached to each of the three Army Commands to insure their "unflinching readiness to fight the enemies of our native land". Stalin also formed special Rear Security Detachments to execute deserters and stop unauthorized retreats.

As the military situation began to improve, the Soviet wartime economy began to gain ground. By 1942, the USSR's production of weapons and ammunition was exceeding pre-invasion levels, and in 1943 the Soviet Union's production of tanks and aircraft was higher than that of Nazi Germany.

The end of the war found the USSR ravaged on a scale rivaling that of the Civil War. The Nazi Army had destroyed 2,000 towns, 70,000 villages and left 20 million dead and 25 million homeless. Russians suffered one-third of the total combat deaths in the war. Factories employing a total of 4 million had been leveled.

At the end of the war, however, Stalin decided to put reconstruction on hold and channel efforts into building up the Red Army's conventional weapons in an effort to offset the United States nuclear monopoly. This increase in military spending led to widespread shortages and placed a heavy strain on the already ruined economy.

By the end of the 1940's, Stalin faced opposition once again. Voznesensky, the head of Gosplan, proposed redistributing the USSR's economic resources more evenly among the various Commissariats instead of placing emphasis on the military and security forces. After Voznesensky proposed new economic measures for the next Five Year Plan, Kruschev, Malenkov and Molotov informed Stalin that they had "seen and approved" the measures. Stalin interrupted, "Before you go on, you should know that Voznesensky was shot this morning. Are you telling me that you, too, are enemies of the people?"

By 1953, the entire Politburo was moving against Stalin, and the so-called "Doctor's Plot", in which various people were accused of trying to poison the Party leaders, indicated that another purge was in the works. Before he could carry it out, however, Stalin had a stroke on March 1 and died four days later.

While Westerners tend to look upon Stalin as nothing more than a ruthless dictator, few understand the role of the Stalinist era in consolidating the neo-colonial revolution. The economic situation demanded the rapid centralization of the economy in order to allow planning for rapid growth through agrarian collectivization and industrialization. This economic centralization could only take place through a central political apparatus that held sole economic control. This pyramidal structure was also perfectly suited for the purposes of a ruthless dictator who could seize it and use his position to eliminate all political and economic opposition. In this manner, the rapid industrialization of the Russian economy was accomplished, and the Soviet Union was able to maintain its national independence despite the challenges of the Nazi era. While the harsh methods of the Stalinist era may not have been democratic or humanitarian, they were vital to maintaining the economic independence of the neo-colony.

With the completion of the collectivization program and the beginnings of rapid industrialization, the purpose of the Stalinist bureaucracy turned from that of building the Russian economy to that of manipulating that economy for the benefit of the ruling bureaucracy. As Djilas points out, "Initially, the state seizes all means of production in order to control all investments for rapid industrialization. Ultimately, further economic development has come to be guided mainly in the interests of the ruling class."

Thus, the petty bourgeois class of managers settled down to the task of exploiting the socio-economic system it had constructed. Within a short time, however, it became apparent that the same economic process that had created the Leninist society had begun the process of its dissolution. The end of the industrialization phase marked the beginning of the decline of the Leninist state.

FIVE : Decentralization (1953 to 1970)

Stalin's death produced a power struggle within the Kremlin, with each faction of the ruling bureaucracy struggling to gain the power lost by Stalin. Eventually, political power over the bureaucracy was split, with Kruschev taking over as Secretary-General of the Party and Malenkov taking over as Premiere.

The ascension of Kruschev and Malenkov marked the rise of the anti-Stalin faction that had begun to assert their influence shortly before Stalin's death. Once firmly in power, the new leadership began to downplay the achievements of the Stalin regime and attempted to erase the influence of the remaining Stalinist hardliners. Kruschev even went so far as to change the name of Stalingrad to Volgagrad.

Pravda, echoing the views of the new rulers, attacked the centralization of political power that had occurred under Stalin, saying, "Decisions taken by individuals are always or almost always one-sided." *Pravda* now called for a "collective leadership" to insure that "citizens' rights are under the reliable protection of Soviet socialist legality and will be sacredly observed and secured by the Soviet Government."

Kruschev, in announcing an end to Stalinist repression, declared, "The Party has always attached tremendous importance to self-criticism, and particularly criticism from below, to uncover shortcomings, and to fight against complacency. Suppression of criticism is a grievous evil, and he who substitutes for it pompousness and bragging has no place in the Party."

To further demonstrate the new policy of relaxation and openness, Kruschev and Malenkov began to release and "rehabilitate" those political prisoners who had opposed Stalin. The new government announced an amnesty for prisoners serving five years or less and a 50% reduction for all sentences longer than 5 years. The only exceptions were those imprisoned for murder or for "counter-revolution". Nine of those convicted in the "Doctor's Plot" were released, and Beria himself, Stalin's security chief, was arrested for "criminal and anti-state activities" in 1953. Beria "confessed" on December 16 and was shot on Christmas Eve.

To prevent the rise of another secret police chief, Kruschev had the Cheka split into two sections in 1954. The Ministry of Internal Affairs (MVD) was given responsibility for internal security, while the Committee for State Security (KGB) was put in charge of external intelligence gathering.

Stalin's political supporters were the next group to arouse Kruschev's wrath. Hard-line Stalinists in the Party apparatus were thoroughly purged. When the new Supreme Soviet was elected in March 1954, over 80% of the old delegates were replaced with Kruschev supporters.

By 1956, Kruschev, the more articulate of the two leaders, had begun to attack Stalin directly. In his "secret speech" to the 20th Party Congress, he attacked what he called the "cult of personality". Stalin, he charged, had committed a "whole series of exceedingly serious and grave perversions of party principles, of party democracy and of revolutionary legality."

> Stalin is no longer living, but we have thought it necessary to denounce the disgraceful methods of leadership that flourished in the circumstances of the Stalin cult. Our Party is doing this to prevent phenomena of this sort from ever being repeated.

Kruschev vowed to "preclude any possibility of a repetition in any form whatsoever of what took place during the life of Stalin."

These attacks on Stalinist methods were not motivated by any humanitarian concerns for the downtrodden masses. In spite of the collectivization fiasco and the war, the stratum of Soviet society that was most devastated by Stalin was the Communist Party itself. The purges had removed huge numbers of privileged bureaucrats and had imprisoned or shot many more. In addition, economic privilege had come more and more directly under Stalin's personal control. Stalin himself decided who in the ruling bureaucracy would get the best of the goodies. The centralized methods of Stalinism threatened to produce another autocrat, and threatened the privileges of the ruling bureaucracy.

Under these conditions, the ruling class had no choice but to attempt to remove the threat. Unexpectedly, Mother Nature removed Stalin before the bureaucracy could, but the new ruling class saw the wisdom of taking steps to prevent another Stalin from appearing. As Milovan Djilas put it, "The new class is tired of dogmatic purges and training sessions. It would like to live quietly. It must protect itself even from its own authorized leader now that it has been adequately strengthened."

Kruschev and Malenkov also attempted to put an end to Stalin's militaristic economic program. Instead of increasing heavy industry and military production, they called for a renewed emphasis on farm production and consumer goods. In 1956,

Kruschev remarked: "Now that we possess a powerful heavy industry developed in every respect, we are in a position to promote rapidly the production of both the means of production and consumer goods; the Party is doing and will continue to do its utmost to insure that the requirements of the Soviet people will be satisfied more fully and better; it considers this its prime duty to the people."

To increase Soviet productive ability, Kruschev began to arrange deals with foreign countries for much-needed industrial machinery. In 1953, the USSR imported nearly $34.5 million from Britain alone, and exported $111 million to the UK. The next year, Kruschev offered to buy some $1 billion worth of British products, largely heavy industrial machinery that had been placed under embargo by the United States, over the next two years. This trend continued, and between 1960 and 1969 the USSR imported almost $1.5 billion in industrial machinery from the West.

The industrial campaign was hampered, however, by several factors. Soviet industry was struggling with obsolete technology, and the bureaucratic maze of the planning apparatus led to waste and inefficiency. The ball-bearing industry alone lost about 57% of its finished product as a result of waste or loss, while the rolled steel industry's losses totaled about 29%.

In addition, the USSR was facing a growing shortage of labor. The tremendous losses suffered in World War II, as well as other factors, steadily reduced the number of workers available for industrial growth. During the 1960's, the Soviets managed to obtain 14 million new workers by transferring domestic workers and surplus agrarian workers to the factories. but these sources were limited. After they had been used up, the labor supply would grow only as fast as the Soviet population, and this was a mere 1% per year.

Kruschev's major emphasis, however, fell upon the sagging Soviet agricultural sector. To increase productivity and produce more consumer-oriented goods, Kruschev began to emphasize the privately-owned plots on the collective farms, which were producing most of the marketed supplies. In November 1951, he removed excess low-level Party bureaucrats and government apparatchiks and shifted them to farm and factory work.

At the same time, he began the ill-fated "Virgin Lands" program to increase the area under cultivation. Nearly 100,000 members of Komsomol, the Communist Party's Youth League, were put to work preparing some 32 million acres of land in Kazakhstan, Siberia and the Urals for cultivation. This ambitious program failed, however, when the climates in these regions proved unsuitable for growing grain.

Kruschev's attempt to improve the Soviet consumer economy, however, soon fell victim to geo-political realities. By 1955, the Cold War was raging, and as Soviet-American relations worsened, each side began preparing for a military showdown. By February 1955, the Communist Party's Central Committee decided to drop the emphasis on consumer production and build up heavy industry and war production to counter the American threat.

At about this time, a power struggle broke out between Malenkov and Kruschev. The more liberal Kruschev rallied his supporters and, in February, Malenkov stepped down as Premiere. His "inexperience" and his "mistaken" emphasis on consumer goods, he declared, had led him to resign his post. He was replaced as Premiere by Bulganin.

To counter the potential threat posed by the formation of the NATO Alliance, the Soviets made hasty plans to expand their own military strength. Faced with a steadily weakening economy, Kruschev sought a way to expand Soviet military potential without increasing military spending. The answer was the 1955 Warsaw Pact, which united the military forces of the USSR with those of the East European nations. The satellite nations, which after the war had become economically dominated by the Soviet Union, now became militarily dominated also.

By the second half of the decade, competition between the USSR and the USA had become less military and more economic in nature, and Kruschev geared up the Soviet economy to keep pace. Once again, consumer production was emphasized to produce a higher standard of living. In April 1956, the Stalinist laws limiting job changes were repealed, and the practice of recruiting quotas of workers from the collectives was ended. "We shall conquer capitalism," Kruschev declared, "with a high level of work and a higher standard of living." With increased economic output, he thundered, the Soviet Union would "bury" the West.

As the Soviet economy geared up for the new economic war, the last remnants of the old Stalinist repression were dismantled. Censorship was lifted and relative freedom of thought was permitted. The Communist Information Bureau, or Cominform, was disbanded. Cominform had replaced the Communist International (Comintern) which had been set up to keep Communist movements in the West in line with Soviet policy. Kruschev curtailed the power of the MVD, and abolished secret trials and deportation to Siberian camps for all but "serious" political crimes.

These liberal measures antagonized a large part of the ruling bureaucracy, including those hard-line Stalinists who remained in positions of power. Molotov, for example, accused Kruschev of weakening Soviet heavy industry and military strength by emphasizing consumer production. Molotov was joined by Malenkov and Kaganovich, and the three attempted to wrest control from Kruschev in July 1957. The attempt failed, and Kruschev removed the "oppositionists" from the Central Committee and had them assigned to minor posts.

Doubts about the effectiveness of Kruschev's programs were erased on October 4, 1957, when the Sputnik satellite was launched. The West was stunned by the accomplishment, and the Space Race was begun in earnest. The Soviet Union, once a backward peasant nation, had to be recognized as a major technological power.

After dealing with Malenkov and Molotov, Kruschev turned once again to dealing with the sagging consumer industries which, in 1958, had accounted for only 28.4% of GNP. In an attempt to increase the marketed food supplies, the compulsory share of produce from the private plots which was taken by the state was abolished. In 1956, the private plots had produced about 30% of total marketed produce. In 1959, private plots produced about 82% of marketed eggs, 70% of potatoes, 50% of meat and 45% of vegetables.

When critics attacked these "capitalistic programs", Kruschev bluntly replied, "It is sometimes very difficult when you have a hungry stomach to understand the theory of Marxism-Leninism."

Kruschev's new penal code, introduced in 1958, struck the final blow to Stalin's excesses. New laws abolished the Stalinist practice of holding the family members of an "enemy of the people" responsible for his actions, shifted the burden of proof onto the prosecution, and outlawed the use of coercion to obtain "confessions". Kruschev also considered dismantling the MVD into 15 separate Ministries at the Republic level, and this was done in 1960.

To the centralists within the Party, these actions were outrageous. While Stalin had attempted to eat all of the candy in the store by himself, Kruschev appeared to be throwing open the doors to everyone. The ruling bureaucracy, terrified and watching its position of privilege slowly disappear, placed Kruschev under increasing attack. In March 1958, Kruschev replaced Bulganin as Premiere, ending the period of "collective leadership" and placing all political power in his hands. Bulganin had supported the Molotov group against Kruschev. Kruschev also replaced the popular Defense Minister Zhukov, charging him with promoting his own "cult of personality".

Now firmly in control, Kruschev began to accelerate his economic program. By 1959, Soviet blast furnaces were producing twice as much steel as similar blast furnaces in the United States, while Soviet electric steel furnaces outproduced the US by 50%. By the 1960's, the USSR was outproducing the United States in coal, iron ore, railroad locomotives, cement, wool and refined sugar. The Soviets were also the second largest producer of watches, surpassed only by the Swiss.

During this time, trade with the West continued to increase, and reached the 10.5 billion ruble mark, compared with some 31.6 billion rubles worth of trade with the East European bloc. Over the next year, trade with the West leaped some 60%. Both Italy and Britain completed trade agreements with the Soviets in 1960. In 1962, the USSR attacked the newly-formed European Common Market, calling instead for "an international trade agency to embrace all regions and countries of the world without any discrimination."

A year later, however, agricultural problems began to take their toll. Crop failures produced shortages and hunger, and the Soviets were forced to purchase grain from Australia, Canada and the United States.

Much of the agrarian problem lay with the lack of mechanization and modernization in the agricultural sector, particularly the area of transportation. In 1964, the USSR had only 700,000 miles of road, of which only 200,000 miles were paved. The United States, by contrast, had 3.6 million miles of road, of which only 900,000 miles were unpaved.

A much larger cause of the Soviet Union's economic problems, however, was due to the sprawling economic planning apparatus, which, by the mid-1960's, had begun to outlive its purpose. The same rigid planning system that had enabled the rapid industrial growth of the 1930's and 1940's was now becoming a burden that was restricting further growth.

As the economy grew larger and more complex, the planners at the top of the economic bureaucracy became more and more removed from the actual economic situation. To facilitate rapid growth, the economy was pushed in a limited number of directions, most notably in heavy industry, military production and space technology, but was allowed to slack in other areas, particularly agriculture and consumer production. In addition, the bureaucratic maze created by Gosplan made it impossible for new ideas or methods to reach the higher levels. The immense bureaucracy was further hampered by Gosplan's reluctance to experiment with new methods.

The practice of emphasizing production output in order to expand the economy rapidly was also leading to problems at the lower levels of the economic hierarchy. Under the central planning system, the overriding incentive for the manager was to produce enough to meet the quota set for him by the Five Year Plan. Managers who met their quota received a bonus, and those who exceeded their quota got a bigger bonus. In 1956, for instance, the director of an oil plant would receive 40% of his salary as a bonus for fulfilling the plan, plus an additional 4% for each percentage point over quota.

The managers realized, however, that if they met their quota too easily, the planners would increase their quota for the next Five Year Plan. To avoid this, most managers held back on production to avoid overfulfilling the quota too easily. Soviet factories made a practice of lagging for several weeks and then doing half of their work during the last week of the month. Other managers met their quotas by turning out shoddy, poorly-constructed products. Considerations such as quality, efficiency or production costs were ignored; fulfilling the Plan quota was the only goal.

The quota system also made it difficult to retool or re-equip factories to meet new specifications or to produce new products. Abandoning one type of refrigerator for another, for instance, meant that the factory had to be shut down in order to re-equip it to manufacture the new product. While the factory was thus idled, production ceased and the Plan was not met. Consequently, factories most often continued to produce what they had always produced, regardless of practicality or usefulness.

New products and processes were similarly resisted by the planners themselves, since their jobs depended on constantly increasing output in their area. Few planners were willing to risk delays and cost increases by introducing new ideas or methods, and were content to continue producing obsolete products using out-dated processes.

Kruschev bitterly attacked this tendency. "The production of steel," he complained, "is like a well-traveled road with deep ruts; here even blind horses will not turn off because the wheels will break. A material appears which is superior to steel, and is cheaper, but they keep on shouting 'Steel, steel!'."

In an attempt to correct the problems associated with the planning system, Kruschev, in 1957, decentralized the system, moving authority from the Glavki level to local economic planning councils. While this streamlining was a step in the right direction, it soon became apparent that more drastic action was necessary. In 1959, Soviet economist Gatovski concluded that "purely administrative methods of control from above" would only continue to bind the economy. He called for a more efficient use of resources by paying more attention to "price, costs, profits" and other factors. Others echoed Gatovski's call for increased economic decentralization.

In 1962, Professor Evsei Liberman put forth the most comprehensive call for reform. Referring to the economic contest with the United States, Liberman concluded that "success in competition could not be gained by the old method of administrative and excessively centralized management." Instead of the rigid control from above that characterized the Stalin era, Liberman proposed restructuring the bonus system and reforming the entire planning system to decrease emphasis on output, making the use of resources more efficient by emphasizing the rate of return on invested resources.

Rather than maneuvering to "beat the system", Liberman argued, factory managers should be free to set their own wages and prices within a general scale set by Gosplan, and should be able to produce for profit within the guidelines of the Five Year Plan. Thus, Liberman wrote, the factory could concentrate on using its resources efficiently, eliminating waste and streamlining the bloated economic bureaucracy. "The proposed system," he concluded, "will free central planning from petty tutelage over enterprises, and from costly attempts to influence production, not economically but by administrative measures. The enterprise itself knows best and can discover its potentialities."

In August 1964, Soviet economist V. Trapenikov, writing in *Pravda*, seconded Liberman's proposal:

It is time to abandon obsolete forms of economic direction, resting on indices and directors, and to transfer to a more simple, efficacious and cheaper form of regulating the work of enterprises. This regulation should be such that the personnel of enterprises are economically interested in developing their work in a direction that is advantageous to the national economy.

The ideal index for regulating the efficient use of resources, concluded Trapeznikov, was profit, representing the amount of money left over after the Plan had been fulfilled.

In 1961, Kruschev began experimenting with Liberman's proposals. Two textile factories were built with programs that were similar to Liberman's ideas. The factories, instead of emphasizing output alone, also placed importance on sales and profits. They neglected, however, to regulate the efficient use of their resources, which Liberman had considered an important measure. Accordingly, Kruschev laid plans to expand the experimental system.

Before he could continue with these plans, however, Kruschev found himself out of power. He was replaced in October 1964 by Leonid Brezhnev as Secretary-General and by Alexis Kosygin as Premiere. The coup had been engineered by Politburo members Brezhnev, Kosygin, Suslov and Mikoyan.

While the reasons for Kruschev's ouster have never been clear, it appears to have been due primarily to political factors. His denunciation of Stalin and his economic decentralization did little to endear him to the old conservatives, while the split between the USSR and Red China, combined with the loss of face at the Cuban Missile Crisis, no doubt convinced the more hawkish Party members that the Soviet Union needed a stronger hand at the helm. Also, the "Virgin Lands" fiasco and the subsequent grain failure cost support among the Party moderates.

In the economic sphere, however, the ascension of Brezhnev and Kosygin changed little. Realizing that the rigid central apparatus was producing economic problems, Brezhnev had no choice but to continue with the decentralization program begun by Kruschev. "There is an obvious need," Brezhnev announced, "to apply economic incentives for the development of production." Kosygin followed by echoing Kruschev's call for increased consumer industry.

Brezhnev first attempted to do something about the USSR's agrarian problems. In 1956, in order to hasten the mechanization of agriculture, Kruschev had begun to emphasize the collective farms over the private plots. Reliance on the inefficient kolkhoz, however, had sparked increases in food prices that brought a tide of discontent in the cities. In June 1962, a 30% increase in meat prices touched off strikes and demonstrations in Novocherkassk. To counteract the problem and keep food prices low, Brezhnev announced that he would reverse Kruschev's policy and use the private plots to increase the food supply.

At the same time, Kosygin searched for ways to shore up the Soviet Union's industrial output. Since the USSR was not able to afford large amounts of Western technology, it had to look elsewhere for sources of financing. Kruschev had also considered this problem and had begun work on a solution.

Until the mid-1950's, the Soviet Union had traded only sporadically with the Third World, usually in raw materials. Shortly before his downfall, Kruschev had begun an ambitious program to increase trade with the underdeveloped nations. To lure them into trading with the USSR, Kruschev offered these nations huge loans that were always made in non-exchangeable rubles. Unable to spend this money in the West, these nations had no choice but to use it to buy Soviet goods. In other instances, the Soviets accepted payment in the form of the country's chief export, leaving it with less to sell to the West and thus driving it into closer economic ties with the USSR. As a result, Soviet trade with the Third World expanded rapidly. While in 1950 the USSR had exported only $32 million to the Third World and imported $93 million, by 1955 this had jumped to 142 million in exports and $160 million in imports. In 1965, the Soviet Union exported $1.2 billion to the Third World and imported $815 million.

This was accompanied by a massive foreign aid campaign, designed to create new markets and sources of raw materials for Soviet industry as well as encouraging friendly relations with the Third World. From 1954 to 1967, the USSR gave out $1.6 billion in foreign aid, compared to almost $52 billion from the United States. American aid, however, was most often in the form of food, medicine or other temporary aid, while the Soviet money went to support such long-term projects as dams, agriculture and industrial projects.

The Soviets also began large-scale sale of military equipment and weapons systems to underdeveloped countries, partly as a way of gaining foreign allies and partly as a way to raise investable currency. In 1966, the 23rd Party Congress decided to increase military spending and temporarily shelve plans to expand consumer production. This was done to counter the new threat from Red China, but also to provide exportable surpluses of military equipment.

At the same time, trade with the West increased steadily. Western nations were the sole sources of badly-needed technology and machinery. As the following table illustrates, Russian trade with western nations, particularly with Italy and Japan, increased at enormous rates:

SOVIET EXPORTS TO AND IMPORTS FROM (in millions of dollars)

W.Germany	1958	1960	1962	1964	1965	1966
Imports	72.2	185.3	206.8	193.6	146.3	135.3
Exports	92.0	160.1	215.0	234.3	275.3	288.2

Britain

Imports	145.5	148.9	161.0	111.2	128.6	141.1
Exports	166.5	209.8	235.5	252.9	333.0	351.8

France

Imports	75.9	115.6	138.1	64.1	72.0	75.6
Exports	94.9	94.7	110.7	141.2	146.0	171.6

Italy

Imports	31.1	78.6	102.3	90.7	98.1	90.1
Exports	40.4	125.8	166.3	147.2	181.3	190.0

Japan

Imports	18.1	60.0	149.4	181.9	168.3	215.0
Exports	22.2	87.0	117.2	266.7	240.2	300.1

By the late 1960's, however, Kosygin noted that copying Western techniques and products was more expensive and time-consuming than simply buying them outright. As a result, trade with the West was accelerated even further (along with an increase in industrial espionage to determine Western technological secrets). Soviet imports from the West shot up dramatically. Between 1960 and 1968, the Soviet shipping industry alone imported $1.4 billion worth of foreign technology. The chemical fertilizer industry imported another $1.2 billion, while the timber industry imported about $630 million, mostly from Japan. During the same period, the textile industry imported $360 million, the food processing industry imported another $315 million, and the metallurgy industry $270 million.

The opening of the Russian market produced a scramble by the industrialized nations, who were eager to sell to the Soviets and grab a piece of the most lucrative deals. The Italians were among the first to realize that Communist money was as good as any other, and the FIAT company built a huge automobile plant on the Volga River. The British built two large chemical plants in the USSR, while Italy and West Germany supplied the technology for a natural gas pipeline in Siberia. The Japanese invested heavily in the Russian timber industry as well as providing technology for mining operations in Siberia.

Despite these sources of economic growth, the sprawling Gosplan bureaucracy continued to produce waste and inefficiency which stunted industrial output. In 1968, the Soviet Union was still spending more on the repair of old machinery than on producing new equipment. To deal with this problem, Brezhnev and Kosygin decided to expand the decentralization experiments carried out by Kruschev.

In September 1965, Kosygin announced that the Liberman plan would be introduced nationwide. The local economic councils were abandoned, and autonomous enterprises were set up, allowing the factory managers to make many of their own economic decisions within the general framework of the Plan.

By 1966, 13 factories were under the new system, and 5500 enterprises, over 33% of the nation's industrial strength, were under the plan by 1968.

This step was accompanied by a series of sweeping economic reforms. Profit and the efficient use of resources was strictly monitored, and the emphasis on output alone was dropped. In order to allow the more efficient use of resources, the factory manager was given more say over the number and use of his workers. Within limits set by the government labor unions, managers were free to employ as many workers as deemed necessary, and were allowed to remove unnecessary laborers. As a result, labor costs dropped by 0.8% in 1966. The work week was lowered from six days a week to five, although the number of hours worked per week remained at 41.

To encourage the managers to be more careful with their use of capital, Kosygin introduced a 6% charge on each firm's fixed and working capital. In addition, Gosbank began charging interest on long-term loans, and rents were charged to mining and other land-based operations.

Towards the latter half of the 1960's, the Soviets began to lay plans for industrial enterprises to negotiate contracts with each other directly, bypassing Gosplan. An All-Union Committee for Material and Technical Supply was formed to oversee the maintenance of warehouses for storing the products of several different Ministries. By 1967, there were over 120 of these, involving over 1000 products, and Planners hoped to double this by 1968. The Soviets also introduced iamarka, or trade fairs, to bring buyers and sellers together without going through Gosplan. In fact, Moscow announced, "The directions of the 1966 to 1970 Five Year Plan call for the gradual replacement of the planned distribution of the means of production by wholesale trade."

An increase in the autonomy of the factory manager was also an important part of the reforms. Managers were given the authority to control the investment of some 20% of the USSR's total financial resources. Each enterprise was granted a Development Fund, paid for by diverting 30-50% of the enterprise's normal capital depreciation costs and a fixed portion of the profits.

In 1960, installment credit had been introduced to encourage consumer spending, and by 1965 some 7% of all nonfood goods sold in the USSR were sold on credit. In July 1967, the pricing schedule was revised, raising the price of coal 78%, oil 230% and rolled metals 43%.

To meet the demand for consumer goods, the Soviets began to study Western commercial techniques. In 1966, the USSR sent a representative to Harvard Business School to research American techniques of business administration. In July 1967, the Soviets held their first International Conference on Techniques of Demand Analysis. Soviet factories began to hire Commercial Managers to anticipate future production requirements.

By the late 1960's, the decentralization process was in full swing. The state planning apparatus remained in control of Soviet heavy industry and continued to set guidelines for economic growth and priorities. The actual day-to-day running of the economy, however, was now largely in the hands of the factory managers. The major thrust of the decentralization program was to remove the restricting bureaucracy that was stifling the expansion of the economy. By 1969, this had been done.

When we examine the decentralization in terms of the class structures of the Soviet Union, however, we can obtain a clearer picture of what was happening. By the late 1960's, it was apparent that the industrialization demanded by the Revolution had been largely accomplished. As we have already seen, this industrialization was impossible without a rigid central planning structure that could organize and direct the meager economic resources which Russia possessed in 1917.

Once this industrialization had been accomplished, however, the central planning system that made it possible was no longer needed, and indeed was becoming a burden on further economic growth. What was now needed was a looser economic structure that could take this industrial base and "fine tune" it by introducing greater efficiency and higher productivity.

It was not possible for the central Gosplan bureaucracy to accomplish this. The economy had grown too large to be overseen in every detail by far-off bureaucrats. If the industrial base were to be fine-tuned, the economy demanded a decentralization of economic power, and the assumption of economic decision-making by a new class that could direct the economy using the criteria of efficiency, productivity and profit. This neo-bourgeois class in the USSR was represented by the autonomous factory managers.

Thus, the decentralization of 1964 was necessary in a historical as well as an economic sense. As the old bureaucratic planning system outlived its purpose, a new stratum of Soviet society, the factory managers, stood ready to sweep the bureaucracy out of the way and assume control of the economy. The 1964 reforms were a first step in this direction.

Of course, the assumption of economic control by the Soviet neo-bourgeoisie could only take place within the context of an assumption of political control. Certainly, the neo-capitalists would not be handed political control by the Leninist state; it would have to be forcibly conquered. It is at this point that we begin to see the necessity of a political and economic revolution in the USSR, a revolution that would sweep away the petty bourgeois bureaucracy and replace it with a neo-capitalist decentralized economy.

The Leninist ruling class, recognizing the economic necessity of decentralization, chose to view this step as merely an expedient to improve productivity and streamline the expensive Gosplan bureaucracy. In reality, it was the first step towards a neo-bourgeois counter-revolution that would sweep away the Leninists. It is, therefore, no surprise that the bureaucracy soon recognized in the economic decentralization the seeds of its own destruction, and took steps to stamp it out.

SIX : Reaction
(1971 to 1985)

The economic decentralization that took place under Kruschev was accompanied by sweeping reforms in the apparatus of the Soviet state. The most spectacular of these, and ultimately the most troublesome, was the relaxation of censorship and the introduction of relative literary freedom. As part of his anti-Stalin tactics, Kruschev allowed the press and the literary world the opportunity to produce books and articles that were openly critical of Stalin's "personality cult". The most famous of these works came to be known in the West as *One Day in the Life of Ivan Denisovich*, written by a then-unknown mathematics professor, Alexander Solzhenitsyn. Solzhenitsyin had served time in one of Stalin's labor camps.

As the decentralization continued, however, the literary movement began to move from merely criticizing Stalin's excesses to launching stinging attacks on the inefficient bureaucracy itself. This movement, composed largely of Soviet writers, professors and other intellectuals, was at first tolerated, since their criticisms were not widely circulated within the USSR. After Brezhnev and Kosygin assumed power, however, manuscripts that were highly critical of the Soviet Government began to appear in the West. In an attempt to halt the flow of criticism, Brezhnev had the dissidents Andrei Sakharov and Yuri Daniel imprisoned in 1965 for sending manuscripts abroad that had been rejected by the Soviets for publication.

The arrests provoked condemnation from the Soviet intelligentsia, and the flow of critical literature continued, passed on by an underground publishing network referred to as samizdat. Faced with a rising tide of criticism that, the Soviets feared, might escalate into open revolt, Brezhnev reversed the liberalism of Kruschev. The anti-Stalin campaign came to an end, and now attention was focused on the "heroic work" that Stalin had done during the war.

This attempt to re-glorify Stalin, however, provoked another uproar among the liberal intelligentsia. More than twenty-five prominent Soviets, including Sakharov (who had played a major role in designing the USSR's first H-bomb), protested against the campaign. When Brezhnev had several dissidents arrested, the liberals responded with a mass rally at Pushkin Square in Moscow. The police quickly rounded up the leaders.

These new arrests were also protested by Sakharov and the others, who warned the Kremlin that a return to the era of Stalinist repression would be "a great disaster". The Politburo, for its part, allowed the Soviet Writers Union to meet for the first time in six years, but, instead of serving as an outlet for liberal criticism, the Union acted as a muzzle on dissident writers.

As the Soviets tried harder to silence the dissidents, liberal anger became more bitter. The dissident poet Andrei Voznesensky declared in 1967, "We are surrounded by lies, lies, bad manners and lies." When the leader of the Pushkin Square demonstration, Vladimir Bukovsky, came to trial in 1967, he defiantly shouted, "I absolutely do not repent of having organized the demonstration. I believe it has done its job, and when I am free again, I shall organize other demonstrations." Bukovsky was sentenced to three years in prison.

The following year, a petition signed by hundreds of Soviet intellectuals condemned the crackdown as "a witch trial . . . no better than the celebrated trials of the 1930's which involved us in so much shame and blood that we still have not recovered." Protests became more widespread after the 1968 invasion of Czechoslovakia. Riots and demonstrations in favor of the Dubcek government were ended by Soviet police.

By this time, Brezhnev had largely taken over power from his fellow "collective leaders" Kosygin and Podgorny. While Brezhnev tried to take care of the problems caused by decentralization, however, some segments of Soviet society were trying to take care of Brezhnev. In 1968, a student shot a Red Army General he had mistaken for Brezhnev during a parade. The would-be assassin was dragged away, screaming, "I did it to wake up Russia."

As economic decentralization gave the Soviet Republics more economic control, several non-Russian Republics began to demand political autonomy as well. In 1968, a rebellion in favor of Lithuanian independence quickly spread to Latvia, Estonia and the Ukraine. As these revolts were being put down, three Soviet Navy officers were arrested for forming a resistance network in Moscow, Riga, Perm, Baku and Khabarovsk. Censors shut down plays that were openly critical of the use of force to end dissent, and the dissident writer Solzhenitsyn was expelled from the Writers Union.

The Soviet Government, recognizing that the wave of political dissent had been triggered by the economic decentralizations, decided that the Liberman reforms were too dangerous and had to be ended if the dissenters were to be silenced. In March 1970, Politburo members Suslov, Shelepin and

Mazurov launched vehement attacks on Brezhnev's economic policies, and attempted to wrest control of the Politburo. Brezhnev, supported by Defense Minister Grechko and KGB head Yuri Andropov, managed to rally his forces and stay in control, but he too had seen the light. Economic decentralization could not be accomplished without provoking cries for political decentralization as well. Since this was unacceptable to the ruling bureaucracy, the Liberman reforms were repealed and decentralization was ended.

In order to placate the restless intelligentsia and defuse popular resentment, Brezhnev announced that the 1970 to 1975 Five Year Plan would greatly increase the production of consumer goods. "The main task of the Five Year Plan," he declared, "is to insure a considerable upswing in the material and cultural standards of the people." The new Plan called for a 20% increase in food production and a 4% increase in consumer goods. In addition, industrial workers were to receive a pay increase of 1% per year; agricultural workers would get a raise of 6% per year. The decentralized Plan of 1965 to 1970, under which production targets had to be lowered twice, gave way to the heavily centralized 1970 to 1975 Plan.

Economically, the new Five Year Plan began on a successful note, as industrial output rose 8% in 1970. Politically, however, the Plan did nothing to silence the wave of dissent. In February 1970, four Western students were arrested for passing out anti-Soviet leaflets. Three months later, Soviet biologist Zhores Medvedev spoke out against the government's practice of censoring the mail of suspected dissidents. Medvedev was arrested and, in a favorite Soviet tactic, was confined in a mental institution. Shortly after Medvedev's arrest, Sakharov helped to found the Human Rights Commission to unify the growing dissident movement. The Commission urged the Politburo to "restore democracy and freedom".

The dissident movement soon began to aggravate the economic problems that were already present within the system. The Soviet scientific community and the industrial sector were so cut off from each other by a maze of Ministries and bureaucrats that most of the Soviet Union's scientific discoveries never found their way into use. As a result, the Soviet Union was falling far behind the West in such high-tech areas as computer technology, telecommunications, cybernetics and petrochemicals. Because of this lack of technology, the average Soviet worker's productivity fell 50% below that of the average American, and a Soviet farm worker produced only 20% of the output of his American counterpart.

Furthermore, the dissident movement and the economic problems had produced a large number of Soviet Jews who wanted to emigrate to Israel. For the Soviets, faced with economic chaos and a severe labor shortage, the loss of this many skilled workers was unacceptable, and the Jews were not allowed to leave. This decision brought condemnation from the West and from the liberal Soviet intellectuals.

By 1971, the huge Soviet military industry was beginning to become a drain on the already-strained economy. When the United States agreed to detente, the opportunity was seized by both the USA and the USSR to cut back on their military expenditures and to deal with their respective domestic dissent. When the Soviet dissident movement called for another demonstration in Pushkin Square, it had become so weakened by arrests that only 25 demonstrators showed up.

Nevertheless, the return of the centralized Gosplan apparatus had brought with it the return of waste and inefficiency. Nearly half of all the glass produced in the USSR in 1971, for instance, was broken during shipment. The Soviet Union employed 26% of its population in agriculture, compared to only 2% in the US. Yet one American farmer was able to feed 59 people — a Soviet farmer could feed only 8. The 1972 harvest was a disaster and fell some 30 million tons short. This forced the USSR to buy $750 million worth of grain over the next three years and pushed the Soviet trade deficit to $600 million. Furious, Brezhnev fired Agricultural Minister Matskevich, who had earlier headed Kruschev's disastrous "Virgin Lands" program.

Things were not much better in the industrial sector. The Soviet mining industry, which chewed up 40% of the country's labor force and 25% of its invested resources, was a dismal failure. Only 2-3% of the USSR's obsolete machinery was being replaced each year. As a result, industrial output for 1972 rose only 6.5%, not the planned 6.9%. The Soviet Union's GNP rose only 2%, the worst since World War II.

In March 1972, Brezhnev admitted that the new factories which were to produce the increase in consumer goods called for in the Plan had not even been built yet. To meet the targets of the Five Year Plan, the number of different types of refrigerators to be produced was cut from 26 to 6, and the number of kinds of washing machines dropped from 32 to 6. In December, the Kremlin cut the projected growth in consumer industry for the year from 8.1% to 4.6%. This came as no surprise to the Soviet consumer, who had been faced with shortages of consumer goods all year round.

The economic downturn provoked protests and strikes. Dissidents began to pass out leaflets charging the Kremlin with wasting money and resources by manufacturing weapons for the Eastern Bloc and luxury items such as caviar and vodka for the West, instead of producing bread and meat for the Soviet population. In June 1972, demonstrations in Lithuania were again put down by the Soviets.

As the economic situation grew worse, the Soviets increasingly turned to the West for aid. In October 1972, a new USSR/USA trade agreement was reached. Three months later, *Pravda* was praising trade with the West as "a promising way of raising efficiency".

Between 1972 and 1973, Soviet imports from the West shot up 60% to $2.7 billion, of which $500 million came from the United States. In March 1973 the Export/Import Bank extended $101 million in credit to the Soviet Union, largely to pay for a truck and engine plant on the Kama River. In addition, the Soviets were forced to sell some 200 tons of gold to pay for their imports.

During the 1973 OPEC oil embargo, the USSR made a killing by selling oil to the US, Belgium and the Netherlands, but this gain was nullified by the 1973 Arab-Israeli War. The war not only cost the USSR its American financing and imports, but also forced the Soviets to pay $5-10 billion to re-arm their Arab allies.

In order to cut its losses, the Soviets embarked on a crackdown on illegal economic activities. The flourishing black market constituted a vast underground economy where millions of rubles exchanged hands.

The black market was particularly active in Georgia, and Soviet official Eduarde Shevardnadze was dispatched to the area. What he found completely amazed him. A sporting goods manufacturer had, he found, invented several phony employees and grew rich on the "wages" paid to the non-existent workers. Another manager had been secretly running his factory during holidays and kept the profits. Shevardnadze found still another manager who made millions of rubles by siphoning off sweaters and raincoats and selling them on the black market.

During this time, dissidents increased their attacks on the government. They were joined by Soviet Jews who renewed their demands to be allowed to leave, and by Ukrainian nationalists calling for independence from Moscow. Brezhnev ordered Solzhenitsyn deported to Switzerland in February 1974, and arrested other dissidents.

Meanwhile, economic problems continued. Despite the raise given them by the Plan, agrarian workers still received about 40% less than industrial workers. This inequality resulted in a steady flow of laborers from the farms to the cities, aggravating the problems already faced by the collective farms.

In April 1973, after more problems with China, emphasis was again shifted from consumer production to military hardware. New attempts were made to stimulate the sluggish economy through trade with the West. When the United States dawdled on a proposed Siberian natural gas pipeline, the Soviets turned to the Japanese and the West Germans instead.

Within a year, West Germany, Japan, the US and France had all signed new trade agreements with Moscow, and the Americans and French offered huge loans at 6% interest to stimulate trade. Western exports to the Communist Bloc went from $21.7 billion in 1973 to $31 billion in 1971, while Soviet exports rose from $4.8 billion to $7.5 billion. The USSR received so much credit from foreign banks that, by 1974, it was using 20% of its foreign exchange just to pay off its debt.

The greatest economic growth, however, came in the area of the private economy, both legal and illegal. Western experts estimated that some 50% of the fruits, 10% of the vegetables and 40% of the meat marketed in the Soviet Union in 1971 were sold in the officially-sanctioned private markets, and the volume of goods sold on the illegal black market was probably higher. In mid-1974, the Soviet Government began subsidizing the prices of consumer goods in order to avoid price increases that would have touched off strikes.

By the mid-1970's, problems were getting worse. The total Soviet GNP in 1975 was $750 billion, but 13% of this went to the military. The Russian agricultural sector took up 30% of the labor force and 26% of invested resources, but the harvest was still short by 30%. The labor shortage was becoming critical, and the only method of increasing productivity seemed to be through high-tech equipment available only in the West. Runaway inflation in the West, however, had driven the prices of these products to astronomical levels. Nevertheless, the Soviets imported another $9.1 billion worth of technology and sold another 200 tons of gold to pay for it.

By late 1975, the Soviet oil industry was finally providing large amounts of marketable surplus, making the USSR the world's largest producer of oil. By selling its oil at OPEC prices, the Soviet Union was able to ease its trade deficit and earn enough currency to buy Western technology. This, along with increased credit from Western banks, enabled the Soviets to purchase over 1000 complete factories, along with their technical staffs, as well as some $1.5 billion worth of Japanese and German chemical technology. Within a year, however, the Soviet foreign debt stood at $15 billion, and most banks were refusing to extend any more credit.

With the plentiful 1976 harvest and an increase in consumer goods production, Brezhnev once again attempted to improve the efficiency of the Soviet economy. In November 1976, the new Five Year Plan was unveiled, which, Brezhnev announced, would "fundamentally improve" the economy. The Plan proposed to reduce actual growth in nearly every sector of the economy, but would focus heavily on productivity and efficiency. To solve the agrarian problems once and for all, a huge investment, nearly 33% of the total, would be poured into the collectives.

No sooner had Brezhnev announced a new campaign against the black market, however, than revolts broke out in Georgia. Georgian nationalists, angered by the 1972 crackdown, found support among the Georgian peasants, most of whom were involved in the black market. A wave of arson and bombings swept across Georgia, provoking similar rebellions in the Ukraine, Lithuania, Estonia and Uzbeckistan.

While the USSR's staggering foreign debt and its $1.4 billion trade deficit hampered efforts to increase economic growth, other factors lowered productivity in Soviet industry. By 1977, the Soviets were being hampered by a lack of oil reserves. While the USSR had made nearly $3.7 billion from its sale of oil in the 1970's, its own use of oil had nearly doubled. The Soviet oil and mining industry was unable to meet the rising demand.

The Soviets launched a desperate attempt to increase its foreign trade and produce currency reserves with which to purchase badly-needed Western equipment. The USSR established a network of insurance firms, leasing companies, maritime agencies, banks, raw materials companies and various other enterprises all over Asia, Europe and the United States. By 1978, the Soviets had 84 companies in 26 countries, including 40 firms and 13 subsidiaries in the West -- 10 of these in the United States. The Moscow Narodni Bank in London had assets of $2 billion in 1977.

Between 1977 and 1978, the Soviet shipping industry increased over 1,000%. In 1976, 10% of all the cargo shipped between the American West Coast and Hong Kong went on a Soviet ship. A year later, one tenth of the cargo between Europe and Hong Kong went on Soviet shipping lines. The Soviets refused to join the World Trade Conferences and charged prices 25% lower than those set by the Conferences. As a result, Soviet shipping and insurance companies covered 97% of the trade between the USSR and Japan, 75% between the USSR and West Germany and 84% of Soviet/British trade.

Despite these spectacular gains, domestic production still limped along. Productivity was set back by worker absenteeism, wasted labor and the labor shortage. The production of consumer goods was unable to meet demand, and most consumers put their money in the bank, creating an increased demand for future goods that the economy had little chance of providing. In 1978, savings accounted for almost 70% of the USSR's retail economy.

Nevertheless, some consumers had made gains. Between 1970 and 1976, the number of private automobiles in the Soviet Union increased over 600%, although less than 4% of the population owned a car. In 1965, only 21% of Soviet families had a washing machine, only 11% had a refrigerator and 21% had TV. By 1978, these percentages had gone up to 70%, 60% and 80% respectively.

Indeed, despite the economic mess, the upper sections of the ruling bureaucracy lived quite comfortably. High-ranking government and Party officials paid a maximum tax rate of 13%, received one month's salary tax-free each year, and received eight to ten times the average Soviet monthly salary. Those minor officials who oversaw trade with the West were rewarded with fine homes and material luxuries. Even the average citizen benefited from a 1% increase in wages at a time when the price index actually fell 0.4%.

These low prices, however, were maintained by a massive subsidy of $46 billion per year that drained the economy and slowed economic growth. Agricultural growth, which had averaged 6% per year in the first half of the decade, was now down to 4%.

Dissent was still widespread, although the brutally repressive methods of the Stalin era had disappeared. As one Western diplomat said in 1978, "I'd say the biggest change in the past 15 years is the way the secret police have been curbed. Justice is still a very qualified notion, but my impression is that most people no longer fear the midnight knock on the door." The number of prisoners in the labor camps, in fact, had dropped from a high of about 10 million in the 1930's to about 20,000 in the 1970's. As one dissident noted, the treatment of political prisoners was very different than it had been in Stalinist days; "The KGB doesn't torture people anymore to get confessions. When they question you, they never even lay a hand on you now. In fact, the prisoner even has a right to ask for a lunch break now."

This apparent gentle touch, however, did not reduce the effectiveness of the Soviet political police. Rather than resorting to the Stalinist practice of physically eliminating dissent, the modern police simply sever the links between the dissidents and the people. This was usually done by exiling the dissident to a remote place within the USSR or in another country, or by secluding the prisoner in a place from which he can have no contact with the outside world, such as a mental ward.

Nevertheless, economic and ethnic conflicts continued to plague the Soviet Union. During the 1979 invasion of Afghanistan, at least one Red Army private was reportedly insulted by a Russian officer who referred to him as an "Uzbek dog". The enraged private promptly shot the officer. The December 1979 Afghan War also provoked protests within the USSR. To deal with these new outbursts, Brezhnev had Sakharov exiled to the remote city of Gorki in January 1980, and attempted to improve his political position by appointing Nikolai Tikhinov as Premiere. Before he could do much else, Brezhnev died in November 1982.

Brezhnev was succeeded by former KGB head Yuri Andropov. Andropov, after surrounding himself with younger advisors, announced that he would institute new economic reforms that would alter the system but leave the central planning apparatus intact. Whether or not Andropov intended to introduce another try at decentralization will never be known. Andropov himself died in February 1984, and was replaced by former Brezhnev supporter Konstantin Chernenko. Chernenko scrapped Andropov's plans and continued the Brezhnev policy of conservatism and reaction.

The stagnation of the economy, however, grew worse, and it became obvious that the old system could not continue in its present form. In March 1985, Chernenko died and was replaced by Mikhail Gorbachev, an economic reformer who had previously served as Minister of Agriculture. Gorbachev announced that he would make economic reform his primary goal. No one, however, could foresee the far-reaching impact that would result from Gorbachev's economic reforms.

SEVEN: Perestroika (1985 to 1991)

From the beginning, it became apparent that Gorbachev's reforms would be thorough and radical. To consolidate his position against the old-line Chernenko and Brezhnev supporters, Gorbachev made sweeping changes in the Communist Party leadership. Andrei Gromyko, who had set Soviet foreign policy since Stalin's day, was replaced by Eduarde Shevarnadze, who had earlier carried out the economic reforms in Georgia. In September 1985, Soviet Premiere Tikhinov resigned due to "failing health", and Gorbachev supporter Nikolai Ryzhkov was appointed as Premiere. Ryzhkov had served as a Deputy Chairman of Gosplan before being promoted to Secretary for Economic Issues by Andropov in 1982. Within two years of taking office, Gorbachev had replaced over half of the high-ranking Party officials with his own supporters.

Gorbachev's primary focus, however, fell on the ailing Soviet economy. Between 1980 and 1985, Soviet GNP had crawled along at an average rate of just 2.2% annually. New investment in productive capacity, which had leaped 11% under Andropov, had slowed to a 5% increase in 1983, and actually shrunk by 1% in 1984. As a result of this neglect, by 1985 depreciation on existing machinery was higher than new investments in production, resulting in a net loss of Soviet productive capacity. In addition, the labor shortage was becoming more severe, and was aggravated by a high rate of absenteeism.

Gorbachev's first actions targeted the productivity of the labor force. Factory managers were given the authority to give employees raises of up to 30%, based on the merits of their work performance. This, Gorbachev hoped, would give workers financial incentives to increase their output and raise productivity. Along with this carrot, Gorbachev also offered a stick. In one sweeping gesture, he closed liquor stores during working hours and inaugurated a campaign against drunkenness. The decline in drunkenness at work produced gains in productivity and reduced the number of work accidents.

Gorbachev realized, however, that much more thorough action was needed, and that the root of the Soviet Union's economic problems lay with the stifling Gosplan bureaucracy. As one Gosplan official remarked, "The latest index of products has 20 million articles. The Plan can't detail that amount." Gorbachev decided that a thorough restructuring of the economy was needed, and he laid out his plans in an August 1985 "Resolution on New Economic Planning". The plan became known as perestroika ("restructuring").

In many respects, *perestroika* was similar to the Liberman reforms which had been introduced by Kruschev. Soviet factory managers were given increased pay incentives and bonuses and were granted more decision-making abilities. Gorbachev's plans, however, were more far-reaching than anything that had been done by Kruschev. Enterprise managers were given the authority to keep and reinvest a portion of their revenues, in some cases as much as 10% of their profits. Under the Gorbachev plan, managers were encouraged to utilize their resources as efficiently as possible, and were given increased authority to set production plans, schedules and amounts of resources used. Gosplan would no longer set the wages and salaries of individual employees, but would merely pass along a labor fund sufficient to cover all of the employees, allowing the manager to distribute wages and bonuses as he saw fit. The Gosplan bureaucracy would be cut in half, allowing individual enterprises to deal directly with each other in obtaining supplies, raw materials and other essentials.

To generate more productive capacity, Gorbachev laid plans to increase capital imports from the industrialized nations. By 1985, the USSR was spending just 10% of its capital outlays on Western machinery and technology. Gorbachev, however, planned to vastly increase this percentage, hoping to utilize high tech machinery from Japan and Germany to increase the productivity of the Soviet economy. In 1987, Gorbachev set up joint manufacturing firms in which foreigners were allowed to own up to 49% of the enterprise. Such joint industrial ventures had been dismantled after the NEP period.

The *perestroika* system was tested in two manufacturing firms, and immediately brought stern protests from the Gosplan bureaucracy. Gorbachev responded by firing Gosplan head Nikolai Baibikov and expanding the system to encompass 25 out of the 51 Soviet Government Ministries and 12% of total Soviet industrial output. The 1986 Five Year Plan called for 50% of the economy to be restructured by 1987, and predicted 4.7% growth in GNP each year. Soviet GNP, Gorbachev announced, would be doubled by the year 2000.

The Gorbachev reforms also provoked opposition from a large portion of the Communist Party, which saw its privileged economic position being eaten away by the increasingly more powerful factory managers. A faction of the Party led by Ligachev attempted to gut the reforms and to curb Gorbachev's power. Gorbachev responded with a bold move designed to cut the Party's hold on the economy. He introduced a number of legal reforms that curbed the power of the Party Secretary General and created vast new powers for the President of the Union (which until then had been a largely ceremonial office), then had himself elected to the new position. At the same time, Gorbachev introduced a campaign of *glasnost*, or "openness", to criticize the inefficiency and corruptness of the Party bureaucracy.

Gorbachev's governmental restructuring had the effect of removing economic power from the Party bureaucracy and placing it in the hands of the soviet apparatus. New election procedures opened up political offices for non-Party candidates and gave the local soviets vastly increased governmental powers. This, Gorbachev hoped, would fill the soviets with factory managers and their supporters, who would back Gorbachev and *perestroika* against the Party and the Gosplan bureaucracy.

During this time, Gorbachev expanded his economic restructuring in new and radical directions. In January 1988, a new State Enterprise Law gave factory managers increased control over the use of employee funds and the reinvestment of profits. By this time, 60% of Soviet industry was under *perestroika*. Enterprise managers were given sweeping powers to negotiate prices with each other and to compete for government contracts, a move which severely cut into Gosplan's powers.

Gosplan immediately fought back by placing government orders which would have consumed nearly all of the USSR's productive ability, thus insuring that distribution would remain in Gosplan's hands, but Gorbachev countered this by limiting government contracts to the areas of defense and consumer products. To increase consumer production, investments were shifted from defense and heavy industry to light industry.

In May 1988, a new law was passed which allowed families and independent traders to set up "cooperatives" for the private sale of goods. These private enterprises were intended to compete with the state-owned factories for government contracts, thus spurring the managers to greater efficiency. A few months later, Gorbachev introduced laws allowing for the rental of farmland to families and granting state economic aid to private cooperatives.

In 1990, the Soviet bureaucrats found themselves under attack in the international sphere as well as the domestic. The process of *perestroika* and *glasnost* had been copied in the satellite states of Eastern Europe as well, but criticism had quickly moved beyond the control of the ruling parties. In a few short months of sweeping rebellion, long-smoldering nationalist resentment at Soviet domination exploded. The ruling Communist Parties of Poland, East Germany, Czechoslovakia and Romania were ousted from power or were forced to join coalition governments consisting of radical reform parties.

Gorbachev hailed the reformers, but quickly became distressed as radical reformist and nationalist movements swept the non-Russian Soviet Republics. In Lithuania, Latvia, Estonia, Georgia and the Moslem Central Asian Republics, mass movements and demonstrations called for an end to Russian domination and the establishment of independent nations.

These secessionist movements represented a grave threat to the USSR, and Gorbachev moved quickly to defuse them. The Soviet economy was extremely dependent on the materials and resources it obtained through the non-Russian republics. The Ukrainian republic alone counted for almost 1/6 of the USSR's GNP, and produced 40% of its steel, 33% of its coal and coke, and 20% of its grain supply. The Baltic republics were the hub of Soviet shipping and transport, while Georgia supplied large amounts of oil and raw materials.

While political control over these "internal colonies" was not important, Gorbachev realized that continued economic domination was vital for the Soviet economy. Therefore, he attempted to defuse the situation by offering the non-Russian republics increased regional autonomy in a restructured Soviet "Federation". Gorbachev also accepted the political and military independence of Eastern Europe, provided that the economic links between them were not severely upset.

By 1990, Gorbachev was facing new internal opposition, this time from the left. Boris Yeltsin, a reformer who favored a program of "market socialism" and the independence of the non-

Russian republics, was elected President of the Russian Republic. Yeltsin opposed Gorbachev's programs and accused him of attempting to become another dictator. Coal miners in the Soviet Union, angry at the slow pace of economic reform, launched a nationwide strike to try and force Gorbachev from power and return power to the soviets. By 1991, Gorbachev was out of power and the Soviet Union itself no longer existed. In its place, a series of Western-style republics had been formed. The centralized command economy was pushed aside by market capitalism in its rawest form, and foreign capital began to flood the new market. The Leninist state had finally met its end.

Since the 1960's, it is apparent, the Soviet petty bourgeois bureaucracy had turned from a progressive force — one that gathered Russia's meager economic resources in 1917 and molded them into an industrial power — to a repressive force that sought to forcibly maintain the state and economic structure which gave it its position of privilege. Forces were already being established which compelled the formation of a decentralized economy and the breakup of the centralized state. These forces were largely economic in nature, and could be neither halted nor reversed by the Soviet ruling class. The only manner in which these economic pressures could be relieved was through the destruction of the centralized economy along with the Leninist state which supported it.

The Second Russian Revolution was, then, inescapable. Circumstances demanded the destruction of the Leninist state and its substitution by a decentralized neo-capitalist apparatus. Significantly, the social sector which could bring about this transition was already well-established in the Soviet economy even before the Gorbachev reforms — the factory managers and the privately-owned cooperatives. These neo-bourgeois classes already held a significant amount of economic power, and as the contradiction between the centralized state and the decentralized economy grew, these classes gained more and more de facto authority. Once the existing state became too great a burden to be tolerated, it remained only to sweep away the old social apparatus and substitute for it a new decentralized one which would allow economic growth to continue.

At first, the aim of these classes is to make the present system work better and more efficiently, to improve its performance and remove its faults. As it became increasingly clear that the centralized planning system has outlived its usefulness, however, and cannot under any circumstances be "repaired" or "improved", the cries of the neo-bourgeoisie turned from "reform" to "revolution".

Gorbachev's *perestroika* was a last desperate attempt to prevent this fate. By increasing the autonomy of the enterprise managers, he was attempting to introduce the decentralization which the economy demanded, while at the same time trying to keep the process under control so it posed no threat to the ruling elite. Despite the devolution of powers such as setting wages and production goals, the Soviet state bureaucracy always attempted to maintain for itself the decisive factor — the ability to set prices. So long as the government could set the prices which it paid for privately-manufactured goods and which were paid for state-produced items, it retained the ability to control the flow of wealth from the producers to the government bureaucrats.

This ability, which was vital to maintaining the privileged position of the Leninist ruling class, would never be willingly turned over to the neo-capitalists. It must therefore have been forcibly seized in a political and economic revolution, an upheaval which swept away the Gorbachev "revolution" and the Leninist state.

CONCLUSION: The Future of Leninism

A study of the history of the Soviet Union points out many factors which are of importance in the study of all "Communist" nations. In fact, three fundamental characteristics of Russia before 1917 may also be found in any other nation that has undergone a "Marxist-Leninist" revolution: (1) a feudalist or neo-feudalist autocratic or totalitarian state, (2) a largely agrarian economy in which land resources are monopolized by a handful of wealthy land-owners, and (3) a small but expanding manufacturing sector which is completely or almost completely dominated by foreign financial interests.

These conditions exist virtually throughout the non-industrialized nations referred to as the "Third World". In these neo-colonies, the industrialized nations systematically drain the native economy of raw materials and labor resources, and manipulate the indigenous economy to serve their own economic interests, much as the British and French dominated and influenced the economic development of the Russian economy prior to the Revolution.

If the economic neo-colony is to free itself from this foreign domination, it must be capable of expelling the foreigners and seizing control of the indigenous economy, and of using its own economic resources for its own benefit. Such a task demands the industrialization of the native economy as rapidly as possible.

Since the native bourgeoisie, crushed and dominated by the foreigners, was too weak to carry out this process of industrialization, this task could only be carried out by a segment of the economy that was anti-capitalist in its outlooks. And, since the development of the neo-colony was being hampered by domination and exploitation by foreign capital, this segment also had to be nationalist and anti-imperialist.

Finally, since growth through competition of private capital-owners would at best produce a painfully slow growth and would at worst lead to the re-introduction of foreign capital and subsequent domination, this segment of the economy also had to advocate rapid industrialization through a centralized state-owned command economy. This segment of the economy is the urban small-business owner and the professional intelligentsia. Its political representative is the Leninist Party.

In order for the Leninist state, after the Revolution, to direct the expansion of the economy, it must concentrate in its hands all economic resources, through confiscation and nationalization. Agriculture is collectivized to allow mechanization and to allow the state to extract a surplus for investment in industrial development. The central planning bureau produces economic schedules which bring about the rapid growth of heavy industry. The entire social and political life of the nation is subordinated to the tasks of fulfilling the Plans and industrializing the economy. After a period of time, the collectivization and industrialization plans produce the industrial development which the Revolution demanded. At this point, the Leninist state turns from a progressive force for economic development into a reactionary one that exists merely to safeguard its privileged position.

The central planning apparatus outlives its purpose, and the bureaucratic control and regimentation which enabled the economy to expand so swiftly now acts as a brake on further growth and development. The only possible solution is a decentralization of the economic apparatus, which produces a separate manager class which is hostile and antagonistic to the interests of the ruling state apparatus. The conflict deepens until the manager class is strong enough to bring down the Leninist state, destroying it and substituting in its place a Western-style republic with a capitalist economy.

Thus, contrary to the assertions of those who claim that Leninism collapsed because it "doesn't work", the system fell precisely because it *did* work — it produced the mechanization and modernization which was demanded by historical and economic circumstances. By constructing the industrial base which is needed for success in a world economy, the Leninists have completed their task, and now must give way to a new economic structure, one which is capable of taking this industrial base and expanding it to global proportions.

All of the neo-colonies in the Third World have an urgent need for a similar expansion of their industrial base if they are ever to throw off the domination of the foreigners and become an independent economy, and, as we have seen, the Leninist process is unparalleled for expanding industrial output at the swiftest possible rate. This, in turn, forces us to consider whether the process of Leninist industrialization will eventually be undertaken by all of the Third World.

It is apparent that this will not happen. In order for a Leninist transformation to take place, it is necessary that the neo-colony possesses sufficient resources which will allow it to develop independently of the foreign capitalists. The Soviet Union, for instance, was completely cut off from all foreign sources of investable funds, and was forced to plan and carry out its development using only indigenous sources and materials. In this manner, they avoided the danger of opening the door for renewed domination of the economy by predatory foreign capital.

Any successful Leninist development, therefore, can only take place in nations which possess sufficient resources for their own development but which are prevented from undertaking this task by the interference of foreign capital. Only a handful of the neo-colonies have sufficient indigenous resources to do this. In any other nation which attempts a Leninist development, the lack of indigenous resources will lead to reliance on foreigners to obtain necessary materials, and this will inevitably lead to economic dependence. Such neo-colonies can trade dependence on one power bloc for dependence on another, but they cannot build an independent economy.

Contrary to what the Leninist idealists would have us believe, Leninism is not the ideology of international socialism. It is instead the ideology of revolutionary nationalism, fueled by the desire to free the nation from the domination of the industrialized countries. Leninism does not describe the transition from capitalism to socialism to communism. It is instead a method of moving a neo-colony from feudalism to state capitalism and thence to bourgeois capitalism, from the rule of the landed aristocracy through the rule of the state bureaucrat to the rule of the capital-owner. It is a system which is born from the contradictions of a dying feudal system and a rising capitalist system which is too weak to take its place.

Leninism will not, as Lenin believed, lead to the world-wide socialist revolution. Communism is impossible in any one country, and any socialist revolution must take place in all the countries of the world at more or less the same time, so that each nation's revolution is supported by and dependent on that of other nations.

Nevertheless, since the process of Leninist revolution is so perfectly suited to the economic needs of the Third World, it is unlikely that Leninist revolutionary nationalism will disappear as an ideology or as a revolutionary program. As long as conditions in the neo-colonies remain as they are, Leninist rebellions will be unavoidable. Even the downfall of the Soviet Union will not bring with it an end to Leninist revolutions.